GAME CHANGERS

The Greatest Plays in
NEW YORK GIANTS HISTORY

John Maxymuk

TRIUMPH
BOOKS

There are Giants in my home and heart;
their names are Suzanne, Katie, and Juliane.

Triumph Books and colophon are registered trademarks of Random House, Inc.

Library of Congress Cataloging-in-Publication Data

Maxymuk, John.
  Game changers : the greatest plays in New York Giants history / John Maxymuk.
     p. cm.
  ISBN 978-1-60078-410-1
  1. New York Giants (Football team)—History. 2. Football—New York (State)-New York-History.
I. Title.
  GV956.N4M36 2010
  796.332'64097471—dc22

                         2010012960

This book is available in quantity at special discounts for your group or organization. For further information, contact:
  Triumph Books
   542 South Dearborn Street
   Suite 750
   Chicago, Illinois 60605
   (312) 939-3330
   Fax (312) 663-3557
   www.triumphbooks.com

Printed in China
ISBN: 978-1-60078-410-1
Design by Sue Knopf/Patricia Frey
Page production by Patricia Frey
Photos courtesy of Getty Images unless otherwise indicated

Contents

Foreword *by Tiki Barber*   iv

Chapter 1: Coming Through When It Mattered Most   3

Chapter 2: On the Offensive   41

Chapter 3: The Best Offense Is a Good Defense   87

Chapter 4: The Agony of Defeat   121

Acknowledgments   156

Foreword

One of my goals in pro football was to walk away from the game on my own terms when it was time for me to move on to the next phase in my life. I loved the thrill of playing football and loved playing for the New York Giants; in fact, some people called me "New York City's New York Giant" because I was one of the few players who actually lived in the city. In 10 years, I had stepped up from being a second-round draft pick who was "too small" to being the Giants' all-time leading rusher and receiver. However, by retiring at the top of my game in 2006, I was able to walk, not hobble, away from the game I loved.

In some ways, I had already said good-bye to the game the previous season after the passing of the team's two patriarchs, Wellington Mara and Robert Tisch, who were mentors and father figures to me. The Mara family founded the Giants, so Wellington had been around from the beginning. He liked players who went all out at all times so we got along well, and he always supported me even in tough times. I went to visit his bedside the day before he died to thank this great man for all he had done for me. I was the last Giants player to see him, and days later I led the team into St. Patrick's Cathedral for his funeral services. That Sunday

I was spurred on to have one of my biggest days in his honor, rushing for 206 yards as we beat the Redskins 36–0 at the Meadowlands. Just two weeks later, co-owner Bob Tisch died after a long battle with cancer. Bob had helped this country boy to fit into the flow of the city in innumerable ways. Again, I was the last player to visit his bedside the day before his death and got to pay tribute to the role he played in my life by speaking at his funeral. On the field, we went 11–5 that year, but lost a frustrating five-turnover game to Carolina in the opening round of the playoffs.

Even with the abrupt postseason departure, the team seemed to be on the upswing. I was 31 and thinking of retiring, but I came back for one more run at a Super Bowl victory in 2006. Because of injuries and an inconsistent offense, we came into the season finale with a 7–8 record (after a 6–2 start) and needed to beat my childhood favorites, the Redskins, in Washington to make the playoffs. Big players step up to make big plays in big games, and I had the biggest game of my life in the last regular-season game of my career near my hometown. I rushed for a team-record 234 yards and would not be stopped as I ran right through tacklers. My first touchdown was a 15-yard burst that gave us the lead for good in the second quarter. I scored again from

55 yards out in that same period and then scored the clinching touchdown with a 50-yard run in the fourth quarter. We won 34–28 and were in the play-offs. The next week we lost by three points on the last play of the game to our old rivals, the Eagles, and just like that my football career was over. After the fierce battle, Philadelphia's hard-hitting All-Pro safety Brian Dawkins made a point of finding me to call me a "warrior," his ultimate term of respect. We had faced off against one another in many big games over the years, so his words meant a lot to me.

A few years earlier, versatile Hall of Fame Giants halfback Frank Gifford, who went on to have a long and successful career as a broadcaster, paid me a compliment of similar esteem. Like me, Frank retired as the Giants' career leader in both rushing and receiving. He was the most recognized and revered Giant of his era, and when he introduced me to a group of his old teammates, he called me a "throwback" with "a lot of class." It was his way of recognizing me as part of the Giants' long winning tradition, and I welcomed that accolade. There was nothing better than playing for the Giants organization and representing the greatest city in the world, and I was pleased to be part of the team's rich history.

In the following pages, the whole of New York Giants history is described through the most memorable game-changing plays, from Ken Strong's touchdown run in sneakers for the 1934 title to the David Tyree catch that inspired another New York championship 73 seasons later. This book brings to life the most exciting plays by some of the greatest players in Giants history, including Y. A. Tittle, Frank Gifford, Lawrence Taylor, Phil Simms, and even a powerful tailback from Virginia with a twin brother named Ronde. These players and legendary coaches such as Steve Owen, Tom Landry, Vince Lombardi, and Bill Parcells enriched and embellished the glorious heritage of the New York Giants; I was proud to be a part of that continuum.

—Tiki Barber

Coming Through When It Mattered Most

Wide receiver Plaxico Burress hauls in the game-winning touchdown pass to complete one of the greatest upsets in Super Bowl history.

February 3, 2008

Smacked, Whacked, and Sacked

Undefeated Patriots Are Upset By Road Warrior Giants in Super Bowl

Just five weeks earlier, the 15–0 New England Patriots and the 10–5 Giants had met in a memorable regular-season finale between two teams seemingly headed in opposite directions: the undefeated Patriots toward immortality and the inconsistent Giants toward a third straight quick playoff exit. Even after winning three playoff games on the road to advance to the Super Bowl, the Giants were still 12-point underdogs to the "invincible" Patriots in their quest for the Vince Lombardi Trophy. However, the battle-tested Giants were confident; wide receiver Plaxico Burress even predicted a 23–17 victory. In the other locker room, quarterback Tom Brady scoffed at the notion that New England would score just 17 points; by the end of the game, Brady would be hoping for that many.

As the game got underway, it was clear that the Giants had lost no momentum during the two-week break after the conference championship. New York took the opening kickoff and marched 63 yards in 16 plays to take a 3–0 lead on a Lawrence Tynes field goal. This masterful mix of runs and passes consumed

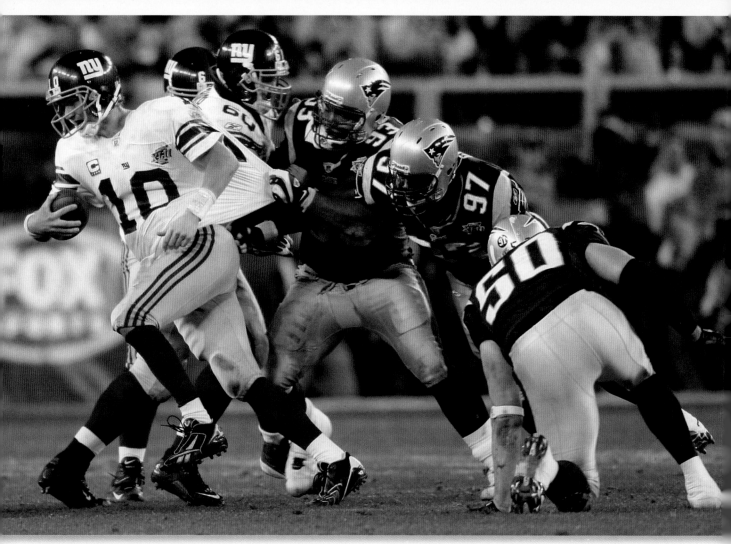

Arguably the greatest play in Giants history began with quarterback Eli Manning miraculously escaping the grasp of Patriots lineman Richard Seymour...

the first 9:59 of the game and set a Super Bowl record for the lengthiest drive in history. Of most importance, it kept New England's offense, the highest scoring in NFL history, off the field. The Patriots used up the rest of the first quarter with their own 56-yard touchdown drive, scoring on the first play of the second quarter to go up 7–3.

The furious pass rush the Giants generated from their front four and occasional blitzers roughed up Brady and kept him out of rhythm by knocking him down 23 times. The Patriots' three second-quarter drives went three plays

for seven yards, three plays for minus 14 yards with two sacks, and nine plays for 38 yards. The last drive took New England close to field-goal position, but Giants lineman Justin Tuck stripped the ball from Tom Brady as he sacked him and the half ended.

The Patriots started to get a little rhythm by shortening their pass routes to start the third quarter. They took 8:17 off the clock and drove to the Giants' 25, but a Michael Strahan sack left New England facing a fourth-and-13 at the 31. Inexplicably, coach Bill Belichick eschewed the 49-yard

...and culminated with David Tyree clutching the desperation pass against his helmet for a crucial first down late in Super Bowl XLII.

field-goal attempt, and Brady threw incomplete on fourth down. The Patriots left a good chance at three points on the field and would later regret it.

After an exchange of punts, the Giants took over on their own 20 to start the fourth quarter with the score still improbably 7–3. Eli Manning dropped back and hit tight end Kevin Boss at the 40 and Boss rumbled another 25 yards before safety Rodney Harrison tripped him up at the Patriots' 35. Three Ahmad Bradshaw runs and a key third-down catch by Steve Smith took the ball to the 5.

Manning's play-action slant pass to fourth receiver David Tyree darted past cornerback Asante Samuel, and the Giants had the lead back with 11 minutes to play. It would not be the last the Patriots would see of special teams ace Tyree.

After another exchange of punts, New England took over on their own 20 with 7:54 to play. Despite having struggled against a ferocious, but now tiring, Giants defense, Brady was not done. Just as he had in his previous three Super Bowls, Brady directed the Patriots on a fourth-quarter drive to take the lead. Three completions to Wes Welker—who tied a Super Bowl record for catches with 11—two to Kevin Faulk, and three to Randy Moss culminated with a six-yard touchdown to Moss with 2:45 to play. The Patriots led 14–10, and time was running out for New York. The unflappable Manning later said, "You kind of like being down four. You have to score a touchdown."

Starting at their own 17, the Giants faced fourth-and-one at their 37 with a minute and a half left, but Brandon Jacobs bulled for two yards to keep the drive alive. Manning scrambled for five on the next play, and then came a forgotten play that could have ruined Manning's reputation for good. On second-and-five, a hurried Manning threw an inaccurate deep out that hit cornerback Asante Samuel right in the hands. Fortunately for New York, the ball bounced harmlessly to the ground, and the stage was set for the play of the day, of the year, of the ages.

On third-and-five from the Giants' 44, Manning took the snap in shotgun formation. The Patriots only rushed four down linemen, but Adalius Thomas came hard from the edge and got a hand on Manning. As Eli stepped up to avoid Thomas, he stepped right into the big push up the middle from Richard Seymour and Jarvis Green, both of whom grabbed hold of Manning's jersey. Somehow Manning broke free and sprinted back five more yards, spotting David Tyree breaking off a deep post in the middle of the field. Manning launched a high floater that Tyree snagged over his head at the 24 while Rodney Harrison swatted at the ball and hooked Tyree's right arm, using his body as a fulcrum to bend Tyree backward in the air. Tyree's left hand came off the ball, but his right hand pinned the ball to his helmet. As the ball started to slip during his descent, Tyree again secured it with his left hand. The brawny Harrison flipped Tyree backward on the ground, still trying to free the ball, but Tyree held onto the ball with a death grip even as he rolled over. It was a 32-yard broken play that left Harrison shaking his head in shock. "There were two or three guys who had [Manning], and he breaks free and throws up a Hail Mary that the guy comes down with," he said.

Game Details

New York Giants 17 • New England Patriots 14

Giants	3	0	0	14	**17**
Patriots	0	7	0	7	**14**

Date: February 3, 2008
Team Records: Giants 10–6, Patriots 16–0
Scoring Plays:
NYG Tynes 32-yard FG
NEP Maroney 1-yard run (Gostkowski PAT)
NYG Tyree 5-yard pass from Manning (Tynes PAT)
NEP Moss 6-yard pass from Brady (Gostkowski PAT)
NYG Burress 13-yard pass from Manning (Tynes PAT)

The Giants still needed a touchdown, though. Manning was sacked on the next play by Thomas and then threw incomplete, forcing another third down. Reliable slot receiver Steve Smith was open once more to convert the third down and stepped out of bounds at the 13. On the next play, Manning hit a wide-open Plaxico Burress for the game-winning score. New England still had 35 seconds, but one more sack, the fifth of the day, and three incompletions ended their last chance. The Giants were champions—they had beaten the unbeaten Patriots in perhaps the greatest upset in Super Bowl history.

Justin Tuck and Osi Umenyiora

While Eli Manning played a fine game and was named the Super Bowl MVP for leading the Giants on the game-winning drive, the real MVPs of the game were Justin Tuck and the Giants' defensive front four, who pressured Tom Brady all day, knocking him to the ground 23 times, including five sacks. Tuck had two of those sacks and also forced a Brady fumble that was recovered by linemate Osi Umenyiora. The Giants led the NFL in sacks in 2007, and Tuck and Umenyiora were the leading sackers on the team, both mentored by veteran Michael Strahan. Although both went to high school in Alabama, Tuck and Umenyiora took widely divergent paths to the NFL.

Umenyiora is a most unlikely NFL success story. He was born in London to Nigerian parents, but his family returned to Nigeria when Osi was seven. At 14, he was sent to Auburn, Alabama, to live with his sister and get an education. He was quite a soccer player and did not play American football until high school. Osi even gave up the game as a senior because his grades were slipping, but he still earned a football scholarship to Troy State, where he earned a degree in business and attracted the attention of the Giants, who selected him in the second round of the NFL Draft in 2003.

With so little football experience, Umenyiora had a difficult rookie season. He did have a breakout game in the season finale, though, with his first sack and two blocked punts. The Chargers noticed his potential and tried desperately to include him in the draft rights deal of Eli Manning for Philip Rivers, but Giants general manager Ernie Accorsi insisted it was a deal-breaker because he valued Osi's pass-rushing talents. Umenyiora rewarded that faith with seven sacks in 2004 and 14.5 in 2005. Hip problems sidelined him in 2006, but he was back at full speed in 2007.

Tuck, meanwhile, went to Notre Dame and set school records for most sacks and tackles for loss. Justin himself was at a loss when he wasn't selected in the 2005 NFL Draft until the 10th pick of the third round. He had a promising rookie season backing up Strahan, but missed most of 2006 to a foot injury. New defensive coach Steve Spagnuolo knew just how to take advantage of Tuck's skills in 2007, though. Despite starting only two games, Tuck was used frequently as a defensive tackle on passing downs and helped create the most fearsome pass rush in the league. Tuck's 10 sacks bested Strahan's nine and trailed only Osi's 13, and led to Justin signing a five-year, $30-million contract extension during the playoffs.

Both Tuck and Umenyiora rely on speed, agility, and moves to get to the quarterback in a hurry. Likewise, both are strong and stout against the run as well, and neither ever quits on a play. Their dominant performance in Super Bowl XLII gave them a national profile.

I felt like I was being grabbed a little bit, but got out of it. Saw Tyree in the middle of the field. I tried to get the ball to him and it just floated. He made an unbelievable catch, jumping up, holding onto that ball.

— ELI MANNING

December 9, 1934

A Strong Run for the Title

Giants Perform Soft-Shoe on Bears in Fourth Quarter

The defending champion Chicago Bears came into this NFL title game against the Giants with a 13–0 record. They had the best offense in the league and their defense was second only to the Lions. The Giants were a good team that finished 8–5, but they had lost to the Bears twice already in 1934, and six out of the last seven times the two teams had met. Furthermore, end Red Badgro was out with a broken leg and tailback Harry Newman was out with broken vertebrae, which he had suffered in a loss to the Bears three weeks before. In their places, end Ike Frankian and tailback Ed Danowski would perform heroically on this icy nine-degree day at the Polo Grounds.

New York scored first with a Ken Strong field goal in the first quarter, but they were nearly run out of the stadium in the second period. Behind a pounding running attack, the Bears marched down the field and scored early in the quarter on a Bronko Nagurski one-yard thrust. Nagurski led the Bears back into the Giants' red zone on their next possession, but the Giants held, and Jack Manders kicked a field goal to extend the Bears' lead to 10–3.

Nagurski next recovered a fumble by Ken Strong at the 6-yard line and then scored on the next play, but the play was erased by an offside penalty. Manders then missed a 24-yard field-goal attempt. Once more, however, Chicago marched deep into Giants territory. Once more, Nagurski plunged into the end zone only to have the play nullified by a penalty, and once more Manders missed a field goal. The Giants were fortunate to go to halftime only down 10–3.

Before the game, end Ray Flaherty told head coach Steve Owen that rubber-soled

The Bears and Giants collided on the icy field at the Polo Grounds in the 1934 NFL Championship Game, forever known as the "Sneakers Game." *(Photo courtesy of WireImages)*

sneakers might provide better footing on the iced-over Polo Grounds surface. Locker-room attendant Abe Cohen was dispatched to Manhattan College to borrow some basketball shoes, since sporting-goods stores were closed on Sunday. At halftime, Cohen returned with several pairs of sneakers, and some of the Giants slipped them on. As the third quarter progressed, the rest of the team changed their footwear during breaks in the action.

The Bears upped their lead to 13–3 on another Manders field goal in the third period, but things began to turn around as the Giants moved the ball to the Bears' 12. But Chicago's Ed Kawal ended the threat by intercepting an Ed Danowski pass at the 4. Ken Strong returned the subsequent Bears punt to the Chicago 30,

though, and the Giants were in business as the fourth quarter began.

Danowski dropped back to pass and appeared to underthrow Dale Burnett in the end zone. Chicago's Carl Brumbaugh got his hands on the ball at the 2, but end Ike Frankian wrestled it out of Brumbaugh's arms for a 28-yard touchdown pass, drawing the Giants within three points of the Bears.

Soon, New York had the ball in Chicago territory again at the 42, and it was Ken Strong's turn. This play offered convincing proof that the Giants were now in control. Strong took a direct snap as the entire Giants line surged straight ahead (with Bo Molenda as the lead blocker from the backfield), shoving the entire Bears line

Lineman John Dell Isola and the Giants switched to basketball shoes for the second half of the "Sneakers Game," giving them a huge edge over the Bears.

Ken Strong

In addition to his 17 points, Ken Strong also ran for 94 yards on just nine carries in this title game. Strong was a triple-threat back who could pass, punt, and kick as well as block and catch. He was a slashing, battering runner who scored 484 points in the NFL, more than 300 of them in his stop-and-go career as a New York Giant.

Strong signed for his first tour with the Giants in 1933; he tied for the league lead in points that year with 64. In 1936, though, he got into a salary dispute with the team and signed with the fledgling American Football League. However, the AFL lasted only two seasons, and Strong found himself banned from the NFL for three years for jumping leagues. After a year with the Giants' Jersey City farm team, Strong rejoined the Giants as a 33-year-old kicker in 1939, but he retired at the end of the season owing to a bleeding ulcer. During World War II, the Giants brought Strong back for a third tour of duty, again just as a place-kicker. After four seasons, he retired for good at age 41 in 1947.

onto its collective back. Strong slid to the left, pushed off the referee standing in his path at the 35, broke a tackle at the 32, and thundered untouched the remaining 30 yards for the go-ahead touchdown.

Another long drive by the Giants was capped by an 11-yard Strong cutback run to the right for his second touchdown. Although he missed the extra point, Strong had tallied 17 points, and the Giants led 23–13. A desperate Bears pass was then nabbed by Molenda, and the Giants took over on the Chicago 22. Four plays later, Ed Danowski slithered in from the 9 to conclude the scoring in this huge upset, which has been known ever since as the "Sneakers Game."

The Giants were NFL champions for the second time, owing their victory to a four-touchdown detonation in the fourth quarter that was at least partly fueled by their change of footwear. However, another advantage for New York in that final period came when their water buckets froze and trainer Gus Mauch substituted swigs of whiskey from paper cups during timeouts. This frigid title game gave everyone a real warm feeling.

Game Details

New York Giants 30 • Chicago Bears 13

Bears	0	10	3	0	**13**
Giants	3	0	0	27	**30**

Date: December 9, 1934

Team Records: Giants 8–5, Bears 13–0

Scoring Plays:

NYG Strong 38-yard FG

CHI Nagurski 1-yard run (Manders PAT)

CHI Manders 17-yard FG

CHI Manders 24-yard FG

NYG Frankian 28-yard pass from Danowski (Strong PAT)

NYG Strong 42-yard run (Strong PAT)

NYG Strong 11-yard run (Strong kick failed)

NYG Danowski 8-yard run (Molenda PAT)

January 27, 1991

New York Clocks Buffalo

Giants Control Ball and Bills in Super Bowl Upset

Super Bowl XXV was a classic matchup of two very different 13–3 teams. The AFC's Buffalo Bills led the league with 428 points in 1990—an average of 27 per game—and were noted as a pioneer of the fast-paced, attack-mode, no-huddle offense. The New York Giants, by contrast, led the NFL by allowing just 211 points during the season, an average of 13 per game. But they had finished just 15th in scoring and were further hampered by having lost their starting quarterback, Phil Simms, to a foot injury in a loss to these same Bills in Week 15. Since then, the Giants had relied on backup Jeff Hostetler and their defense to keep winning games. It was no surprise that the Bills were seven-point favorites in this clash of opposites.

The Giants' plan was simple: keep the ball out of the hands of Bills quarterback Jim Kelly by running the ball and avoiding turnovers. On defense, the Giants often employed just two down linemen, allowing Kelly time to throw but blanketing and roughing up his receivers.

The first quarter ran according to form. The Bills went three-and-out on their opening drive, while the Giants drove 58 yards in 10 plays and took 6:15 off the clock before kicking a field goal. Buffalo answered with a 61-yard bomb to James Lofton that set up an equalizing field goal.

Buffalo opened the second quarter with a 12-play, 80-yard drive, capped by a Don Smith touchdown run, to take a 10–3 lead. The Bills extended that lead midway through the second period when they pinned the Giants on their own 7-yard line. On second down, Hostetler tripped over Ottis Anderson's foot and was sacked in the end zone by Bruce Smith for a safety and a 12–3 Buffalo lead. However, New York's defense stiffened, and the Giants got the ball

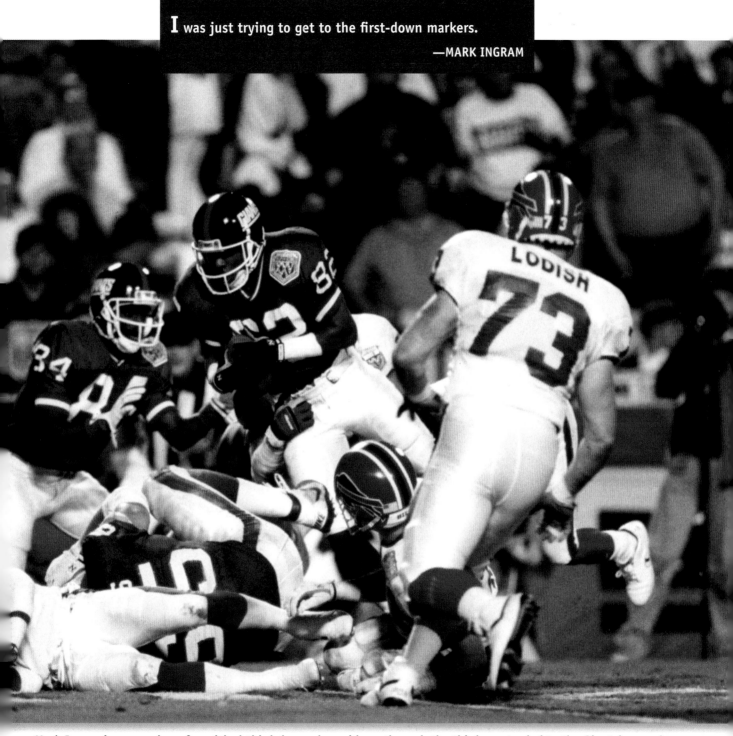

I was just trying to get to the first-down markers.
—MARK INGRAM

Mark Ingram's conversion of a critical third-down play midway through the third quarter led to the Giants' second touchdown and eventual victory over the Bills in Super Bowl XXV.

on their own 13 with 3:49 to play in the period. Hostetler mixed rollout passes and straight drops with an 18-yard Anderson run and a 17-yard Dave Meggett scamper to move 87 yards in 10 plays. The vital score came on third-and-10 from the Buffalo 14, when Hostetler hit Stephen Baker in the corner of the end zone to narrow the gap to 12–10 at the half.

Hostetler was at his best during the opening drive of the second half. Again mixing rollouts, dropbacks, and runs by Anderson and Meggett, Hostetler slowly marched the Giants 75 yards in 14 plays that took 9:29 off the clock, the most time-consuming drive in Super Bowl history at the time. Along the way, Hostetler converted four third downs. The most exciting conversion came on a third-and-13 from the Buffalo 32. Hostetler hit receiver Mark Ingram at the 26, where Ingram spun around converging

Game Details

New York Giants 20 • Buffalo Bills 19

Bills	3	9	0	7	19
Giants	3	7	7	3	20

Date: January 27, 1991

Team Records: Giants 13–3, Bills 13–3

Scoring Plays:

NYG Bahr 28-yard FG

BUF Norwood 23-yard FG

BUF Smith 1-yard run (Norwood PAT)

BUF Smith tackled Hostetler for safety

NYG Baker 14-yard pass from Hostetler (Bahr PAT)

NYG Anderson 1-yard run (Bahr PAT)

BUF Thomas 31-yard run (Norwood PAT)

NYG Bahr 21-yard FG

Jeff Hostetler

In the locker room after this great Super Bowl victory, star backup quarterback Jeff Hostetler was surrounded by teammates joyfully mocking him with chants of "You can't win! You can't do it! You're just a backup!" At last, to the surprise of everyone outside the Giants' locker room, Hostetler had shown what he could do. However, Bill Parcells was not surprised at his success, saying, "We didn't put a rookie in the game."

Hostetler never had a smooth road. Once Todd Blackledge beat him out for the starting job at Penn State, he transferred to West Virginia, where he was an academic All-American and eventually married the daughter of coach Don Nehlen. The Giants drafted him in the third round of the 1984 draft, but he would not throw his first pass until 1988. During his time as the third-string quarterback, Jeff also served as emergency tight end and even blocked a punt. When he took over for the injured Simms in 1990, he had thrown just 58 passes as the Giants' frustrated backup quarterback.

His postseason success led to an immediate quarterback controversy in 1991. New head coach Ray Handley chose the younger and more mobile Hostetler, but Simms still got playing time during the next two unsuccessful seasons. Both quarterbacks found this to be an intolerable situation, so new coach Dan Reeves chose Simms as his starter in 1993 and allowed Hostetler to leave as a free agent.

Hostetler spent four seasons as the starter with the Raiders, throwing for more than 3,000 yards in two of those seasons, but his time there is most remembered for his coach Art Shell sneeringly dismissing him as a "white" quarterback. Hostetler moved on to the Redskins for a season and then retired. As a Giant, he only logged 632 pass attempts for 20 touchdowns and 12 interceptions, but he will always be remembered as a Super Bowl hero.

Jeff Hostetler went from backup quarterback to Super Bowl hero in 1991. *(Photo courtesy of AP Images)*

tackler Kirby Jackson. At the 24, Ingram pivoted and spun in reverse as linebacker Darryl Talley grabbed him by the neck, but Ingram shook loose. Ingram then juked Mark Kelso at the 23, ran right, stopped again at the 21, and spun once more as defender James Williams grabbed his foot. Talley reemerged and dove for Ingram's back as the receiver lunged fully forward to the 18, with Mike Lodish and Chris Hale piled on. Ingram had gotten past six Bills players for the first down in this key play that demonstrated the Giants' determination. The touchdown that followed on a short

Anderson run gave the Giants a 17–12 lead that held into the fourth quarter.

The Bills took the lead back on the first play of the final period, in which brilliant runner Thurman Thomas broke two tackles on a shotgun draw play and scored from 31 yards out. Again, Hostetler bled the clock and moved the ball, this time for 74 yards in 13 plays over seven minutes and 32 seconds. A 21-yard Matt Bahr field goal gave New York a slim one-point lead, 20–19, with 7:20 to play.

Bill Parcells

Bill Parcells's basic philosophy, "Power wins football games," prevailed in Super Bowl XXV. The Giants weren't going to outrun the Bills, but they proved they could overpower them. Unfortunately, it was the last game that Parcells would coach for the Giants. In May, he stepped down somewhat mysteriously, although it later became clear that he was having health problems that necessitated his taking a break from coaching.

The New Jersey native was a perfect fit in the Meadowlands. He began as the linebackers coach and defensive coordinator under Ray Perkins, and he impressed general manager George Young so much that he was quickly named head coach when Perkins left to succeed Bear Bryant at the University of Alabama.

It took a year for Parcells to assert himself and feel comfortable in the position, but once he did, few have done it better. Parcells was a players' coach that established real relationships with each player, treating each one differently as he tried to get the best out of them through various psychological prods and manipulations. It helped that Lawrence Taylor

> **T**he whole plan was to shorten the game.
>
> —BILL PARCELLS

bought into his program, and in return Parcells showed great concern for the off-the-field problems of Taylor and others. Certain tough and gritty players even became known as Parcells's "guys," following the gruff coach from one coaching stop to another.

Parcells returned to coaching in New England in 1993 and took the Patriots to the Super Bowl in his fourth year, but then conflicts with owner Robert Kraft caused him to leave. Subsequent tours with the Jets and the Cowboys brought similar results: he took each team to the playoffs, but was never able to repeat the ultimate success he experienced twice as the coach of the New York Giants. In late 2007, Parcells agreed to become the head of football operations for the Miami Dolphins.

Buffalo was unable to move the ball and punted to New York. The Giants could only make one first down, but they used up three minutes of clock and two Buffalo timeouts before giving the ball back to the Bills at their own 10-yard line with 2:16 to play. As the clock ticked away, New York's suffocating pass defense forced Buffalo to move the ball on the ground. Kelly could only complete two short passes for 10 yards, but three scrambles gained 18 yards, and two Thomas bursts gained 33 more. Kelly spiked the ball at the New York 29 with eight seconds left.

Scott Norwood's wide right 47-yard missed field goal gave the Giants the championship. It was a remarkable team accomplishment by an outgunned underdog. The Giants achieved an astounding time-of-possession supremacy of 40:33 to 19:27 as they choked off the most explosive offense in the league and outgained Buffalo—both on the ground and in the air. New York won behind the labors of its relentless, aging defense; a resourceful, mistake-free exhibit by their backup quarterback, who took a fearful physical beating in the game; and a punishing MVP performance by Ottis Anderson, the oldest running back in the NFL. No player exuded the Giants' fighting spirit more than receiver Mark Ingram, though, whose battling first-down catch in the third quarter exemplified this total team effort.

December 30, 1956

Triplett Tramples Bears to Start Onslaught

New York Ices Chicago for Title

One month before the 1956 NFL Championship Game, the Bears and the Giants met in an odd game in which the Giants were in firm control throughout and led 17–3 with just five minutes to play. However, two bombs to tall, skinny speedster Harlon Hill—the Randy Moss of his day—enabled the Bears to pull out a tie in the closing seconds.

Chicago had the best offense in the league, and they came into the title game favored by three points. A storm hit New York the day before the game, though. The temperature at game time was a frosty 18 degrees and the field was a sheet of ice. Coach Jim Lee Howell's advice to offensive coach Vince Lombardi was to "keep it simple" on this slippery day.

Both teams came out wearing rubber soles, unlike the celebrated "Sneakers Game" between these same two teams for the 1934 NFL title. However, the Giants were shod in new sneakers supplied by Andy Robustelli's sporting goods store, while the Bears were wearing worn-out pairs of practice sneakers that some claimed dated from the 1930s. The

Jim Lee Howell

Kyle Rote told the story of walking down the hall in training camp and seeing defensive coach Tom Landry studying film in one room and offensive coach Vince Lombardi running the projector in another, while head coach Jim Lee Howell sat in a third room reading the newspaper. The self-deprecating Howell often joked, "I just blow up the footballs and keep order." It is true that Howell was a delegator, not a master strategist, but it is also true that he was very successful in that style, as the Giants' 1956 championship proves.

Howell was the epitome of the "company man." He signed with the Giants in 1937 as a 6'5" former basketball star from the University of Arkansas, and spent the rest of his working life commuting between his Arkansas farm and New York. Howell was a starting end under Steve Owen from 1937 through 1947, with three years as a Marine in World War II. He became the Giants' first end coach in 1948 and then succeeded the legendary Owen as head coach in 1954.

Howell ran the team for seven years, achieving a 55–29–4 record and appearing in three NFL title games. When the pressure got too great, he quit coaching and moved into the front office. Howell was the Giants' director of personnel from 1961 through 1979. He then served as a roving scout until 1986, when at last he retired, having spent 50 years with the Maras.

Howell was a disciplinarian with a booming voice who performed his own bedchecks, but he gave a lot of freedom to his celebrated assistant coaches. He liked to say that fourth-down decisions were his responsibility.

> **W**ithout Triplett's blocking, a lot of our plays wouldn't have worked.
>
> —JIM LEE HOWELL

He had no tough choices in 1956, but in 1958 it was Howell who sent Pat Summerall in to try a 49-yard field goal in the snow, and it was Howell who sent Don Chandler in to punt the ball back to Johnny Unitas with two minutes left. One decision worked out and one didn't. The day after the last-minute heroics of Unitas, Howell was photographed in his office shrugging his shoulders, a sheepish grin on his face. He would never again experience the pure elation of December 30, 1956.

Though never a master strategist, coach Jim Lee Howell did lead his Giants to three NFL title games.

difference was apparent right from the start. Giants half-back Gene Filipski caught George Blanda's opening kickoff at his own 7-yard line and smoothly negotiated New York's excellent open-field blocking to return the ball 53 yards to the Chicago 39. Three plays later, on third-and-10, nominal starting quarterback Don Heinrich hit Frank Gifford for 22 yards and a first down at the 17.

The next play demonstrated the Giants' dominance on this day. The Bears showed blitz and Heinrich audibled to a draw play. Burly fullback Mel Triplett took the handoff from Heinrich and burst off guard untouched, as the umpire in the middle of the field turned too late to flee in fear as Mel ran up his back. At the 5, Triplett shoved the umpire forward as defensive backs McNeil Moore and Stan Wallace converged on him from both sides. Triplett dragged the two Bears defenders into the end zone with him, and all three crashed on top of the flattened official. The Giants took a 7–0 lead; they would never trail.

On the second play following the kickoff, Andy Robustelli recovered a fumble by Bears fullback Rick Casares at the Chicago 15. On fourth down, toeless Ben Agajanian converted a field goal to make the score 10–0. Still in the first quarter, safety Jimmy Patton picked off quarterback Ed Brown at the New York 36 and returned the ball 28 yards to the Chicago 36. Again, Agajanian converted the Bears' miscue into three points, and New York led 13–0.

The Bears were getting desperate. After Emlen Tunnell tackled J. C. Caroline for a loss on a fourth-down play, the Giants took over behind the real starting quarterback, Charley Conerly. Four runs and a 22-yard flare pass to Alex Webster brought them to the 3, and Webster powered in from there to start the second quarter. A muffed punt by Tunnell led to the only Bears touchdown, but the Giants answered with a five-play, 71-yard drive that was highlighted by a 50-yard pass to Webster and capped by a one-yard Webster touchdown. To conclude the first half, Ray Beck blocked a Chicago punt and little-used rookie Henry Moore recovered the ball in the end zone for a 34–7 halftime lead.

Game Details

New York Giants 47 • Chicago Bears 7

Bears	0	7	0	0	**7**
Giants	13	21	6	7	**47**

Date: December 30, 1956
Team Records: Giants 8–3–1, Bears 9–2–1
Scoring Plays:
NYG Triplett 17-yard run (Agajanian PAT)
NYG Agajanian 17-yard FG
NYG Agajanian 43-yard FG
NYG Webster 3-yard run (Agajanian PAT)
CHI Casares 9-yard run (Blanda PAT)
NYG Webster 1-yard run (Agajanian PAT)
NYG Moore recovered blocked punt in end zone (Agajanian PAT)
NYG Rote 9-yard pass from Conerly (Agajanian kick failed)
NYG Gifford 14-yard pass from Conerly (Agajanian PAT)

The second half was a formality. George Blanda took over at quarterback for Chicago but engineered no points, while Charley Conerly threw touchdown passes to Kyle Rote in the third quarter and Frank Gifford in the fourth to make the final score 47–7. With the victory secure, Conerly gave way to third-stringer Bobby Clatterbuck. Chuckin' Charley threw just 10 passes on the day, but completed seven of them for an astounding 195 yards. Oddly, the touchdown caught by Rote was the only pass caught by a Giants end all day, but halfbacks Gifford and Webster were free throughout the game. In their first season in Yankee Stadium, the Giants had won their first NFL title in 18 years.

January 25, 1987

Giants Break Broncos

Simms-McConkey Connection Puts New York on Top

It had been 30 years since the New York Giants had won the NFL championship, but 1986 seemed different. New York went 14–2 during the regular season and swept through the playoffs, outscoring the 49ers and the Redskins 66–3 to win a trip to Pasadena to play the Broncos in the Super Bowl. Coach Bill Parcells had been at Yankee Stadium in 1956 when the Giants had vanquished the Bears from start to finish to win the title. Now, with his Giants poised to repeat the feat, he would be fearless and gutsy in trying to win the game.

The Giants had beaten Denver at the Meadowlands in November on a last-minute field goal. There would be much less suspense in Super Bowl XXI. On offense, New York was led by little Joe Morris's 1,516 rushing yards and the underappreciated Phil Simms's 3,487 passing yards. But the core of the team, exemplified by Lawrence Taylor's 20.5 sacks, was its aggressive defense, which gave up the second-fewest points in the NFL.

Sparkplug Phil McConkey led the team onto the field, waving a white towel to get the crowd behind the Giants, but it was the Broncos who came out fastest. John Elway's

first play in the Super Bowl was a 10-yard scramble, and he led Denver on a 45-yard opening drive to take a quick 3–0 lead.

For the run-oriented Giants, Phil Simms surprised the Broncos by coming out throwing on first down; in the first half, Simms threw on nine of 12 first-down plays. Simms was on target, too, hitting his first six passes in the first drive of 78 yards, which ended with a six-yard touchdown pass to tight end Zeke Mowatt. Elway, however, was just as hot. He completed all four passes on the next Broncos drive and scored on a four-yard quarterback draw to take a 10–7 lead, still in the first period.

When the Giants were forced to punt at the outset of the second quarter, though, the game started to turn sour for Denver. Elway drove them to a first-and-goal from the New York 1-yard line, but the ferocious Giants defense dug in and made a memorable stand. On first down, Taylor ran Elway down for a one-yard loss on a sweep. Harry Carson stoned Gerald Willhite up the middle on second down, and Carl Banks nailed Sammy Winder for a four-yard loss on a failed sweep on third down. To top it off, kicker Rich Karlis then missed a 23-yard field goal.

The next time Denver had the ball, Elway retreated all the way to his end zone on a third-and-12 from the Denver 13, and defensive end George Martin corralled him for a safety. Martin was Elway's nemesis—he'd had a 78-yard interception return in the regular-season meeting between these teams. Denver was still able to move the ball, though. Karlis had one more chance at three points with 13 seconds left in the period, but he missed a 34-yard field goal to leave the score at 10–9 at the half.

The third quarter was a Giants onslaught in which they outgained Denver by 161 yards. Simms, who had thus far thrown just three incompletions, would not miss another pass in the game. The opening Giants drive stalled at their own 46, but Parcells sent an unusual group on for the punt. Backs Lee Rouson and Maurice Carthon lined up as gunners

Phil McConkey was upended by Broncos cornerback Mark Haynes, but held onto the ball to set up the game-changing touchdown in Super Bowl XXI.

on the outside, while quarterback Jeff Rutledge lined up as the blocking back. The three then shifted to their normal positions while punter Sean Landeta went in motion as a flanker. Rutledge made sure that the Broncos linebackers were off the line, and then took the snap and made the first down on a quarterback sneak.

Five plays later, Simms hit Bavaro from 13 yards out, and New York took the lead for good. Denver went three-and-out, and Phil McConkey returned the kick 25 yards to the Broncos' 36. Eight plays after that, Raul Allegre kicked a 21-yard field goal to extend the lead to 19–10.

Again, Denver went three-and-out. New York moved to the Broncos' 45, and Parcells sent McConkey in with the play of the game. Receivers McConkey and Bobby Johnson

Game Details

New York Giants 39 • Denver Broncos 20

Broncos	10	0	0	10	**20**
Giants	7	2	17	13	**39**

Date: January 25, 1987

Team Records: Giants 14–2, Broncos 11–5

Scoring Plays:

DEN Karlis 48-yard FG

NYG Mowatt 6-yard pass from Simms (Allegre PAT)

DEN Elway 4-yard run (Karlis PAT)

NYG Martin tackled Elway for safety

NYG Bavaro 13-yard pass from Simms (Allegre PAT)

NYG Allegre 21-yard FG

NYG Morris 1-yard run (Allegre PAT)

NYG McConkey 6-yard pass from Simms (Allegre PAT)

DEN Karlis 28-yard FG

NYG Anderson 2-yard run (Allegre kick failed)

DEN Johnson 47-yard pass from Elway (Karlis PAT)

> **B**obby Johnson was wide open for the touchdown, but McConkey took us to the 1-foot line, so I guess that's OK.
>
> **—BILL PARCELLS**

started out lined up on the same side, but McConkey went in motion to the right behind Mark Bavaro. Simms handed off to Morris. McConkey paused at the line to see if the safety was blitzing and then took off on a 45-degree angle across the field. Morris took two steps with the ball and then turned and tossed it back to Simms. Simms did not see Johnson open by the goal line, but he spotted McConkey and hit him at the 20. McConkey raced for the end zone, but was cut off at the 5 by cornerback Mark Haynes, who went low and sent McConkey spinning head over heels to the 1. Joe Morris powered in for the score on the next play, and with 24 seconds left in the third quarter, the game was essentially over.

The Giants led 26–10 going into the fourth quarter, and Simms would throw just two more passes in the game. His last pass bounced off the hands of Mark Bavaro as the tight end was hit by two defenders. The ball bounded backward—where Phil McConkey was waiting. As he grabbed the ball just a foot from the ground, McConkey likened it to catching snowflakes as a kid in his native Buffalo. But this was a touchdown in the Super Bowl, and his friend Bavaro lofted him in the air exultantly.

In the closing minutes, Jim Burt, who had initiated the practice of dousing Parcells with the Gatorade bucket to celebrate a victory, was celebrating with the fans. In his stead, Harry Carson camouflaged himself in the overcoat of a security guard and drenched his coach with the quenching liquid. Simms, who had completed 22 of 25 passes for 268 yards and three touchdowns in a superlative performance, became the first Super Bowl quarterback to cash in by uttering the line "I'm going to Disney World!" as he left the field. Indeed, he had transformed Big Blue Nation into Fantasyland at long last.

Phil McConkey

Championship teams are made up of many parts: superstars, stars, solid starters, and leaders. However, there is also a need for spirited guys who go all out and take care of the little things. Phil McConkey led his teammates onto the field at the Super Bowl furiously waving a white towel to get the fans behind the team. He set up one touchdown with a 44-yard reception on a flea flicker, and then he caught a touchdown on a deflected pass that bounced off the hands of tight end Mark Bavaro. In fact, Bill Parcells had lauded McConkey as the field-position star of the 17–0 NFC championship win over the Redskins in gusty Giants Stadium two weeks before, for catching every punt and not letting them bounce the way his Washington counterpart had.

The smallish McConkey set receiving records at the Naval Academy in the 1970s but went undrafted by the NFL. Before his five-year navy commitment ran out, he wrote to his hometown Buffalo Bills and the Giants requesting a tryout. New York took a chance on the 5'10" 27-year-old helicopter pilot, and he made the team in 1984 as a return man and reserve receiver. He never caught more than 25 passes in a season and scored only twice in his career, but he was a reliable punt returner who three times led the NFL in fair catches.

In 1986, he fell too far on the receiver depth chart and was cut. When Lionel Manuel injured his knee early in the season, however, Parcells traded a late-round draft choice to Green Bay to bring back the lively McConkey in Week 5. Feisty Phil's inspirational "The grass is greener, my ass" message stayed on the Giants' bulletin board for the entire Super Bowl run of 1986.

Phil McConkey got his Super Bowl touchdown in the fourth quarter, snatching a pass that bounced off the hands of teammate Mark Bavaro.

As I caught the ball and turned up, I saw a wide-open field. I thought I was going to get in. I saw the goal line and thought, *My god, I'm going to get a touchdown in the Super Bowl.*

—PHIL McCONKEY

After missing just minutes earlier, Giants kicker Pat Summerall connects on a 49-yard field goal to force a playoff for the 1958 division crown.
(Photo courtesy of AP Images)

December 14, 1958

Summerall Legs Out a Giants Win

49-Yard Field Goal in the Snow Forces Playoff

The Giants trailed the Browns by a game in the East for most of the 1958 season. When the teams met in the season finale, New York had won three straight and were 8–3 on the year; Cleveland had won four straight and were 9–2. A tie or Cleveland victory would clinch the crown for the Browns. On a cold, windy, snowy day at Yankee Stadium, the Giants had to win.

On the Browns' first play from scrimmage, the Giants' vaunted defensive line and linebackers were completely wiped out, and the great Jim Brown burst up the middle for a 65-yard touchdown run. Brown was not touched until corner Dick Lynch tapped him with one hand at the 30-yard line. The Giants defense solidified after that initial lapse, though, and held Brown to 83 yards on 25 carries during the rest of the game.

The Giants got on the scoreboard themselves in the second quarter with a 46-yard field goal by Pat Summerall, following a fumble by Cleveland quarterback Milt Plum. The Browns' Lou Groza answered with a 22-yard field goal later in the quarter.

Cleveland had the fewest fumbles in the NFL in 1958, but fumbles were what did in the Browns this day. Early in the fourth quarter, Milt Plum lost the ball a second time, and Andy Robustelli recovered it at the Browns' 45. Frank Gifford followed with a halfback option pass diagonally across the field to Kyle Rote at the 10, and Don Paul tackled Rote at the 6. After a failed run by Gifford, the Giants went back to the halfback option play, and Gifford hit Bob Schnelker for the tying touchdown with 10:10 to play.

The Browns would make only one more first down in the game, and they punted back to New York at the 30. The Giants drove inside the Browns' 30, where Summerall lined up for a 36-yard field goal with just under five minutes to play. Summerall missed the kick and felt like the goat. Again, however, the Browns could not move the ball, and Dick Deschaine shanked a 22-yard punt to the Cleveland 42.

As the clock wound down, Charley Conerly threw three incompletions. On one, he hit Alex Webster in the hands in the end zone, but the normally reliable Webster couldn't hang on to the wet ball. On fourth down, offensive coach Vince Lombardi wanted to try another pass. However, Jim Lee Howell shockingly sent Summerall, who had not practiced all week owing to a knee problem, onto the field to try a 49-yard field goal through the swirling snow.

With 2:07 remaining, Conerly took the snap and smoothly spotted the ball on the white field. Summerall made his straight-ahead approach and got full extension from his leg; the ball sailed through the dark, damp night and through the uprights for a 13–10 lead.

Game Details

New York Giants 10 • Cleveland Browns 10

Browns	7	3	0	0	**10**
Giants	0	3	0	10	**13**

Date: December 14, 1958

Team Records: Giants 8–3, Browns 9–2

Scoring Plays:

CLE Brown 65-yard run (Groza PAT)

NYG Summerall 46-yard FG

CLE Groza 22-yard FG

NYG Schnelker 8-yard pass from Gifford (Summerall PAT)

NYG Summerall 49-yard FG

Teammates and coaches mobbed Summerall as he left the field, but the game wasn't over yet. Jim Brown returned the kickoff to the Browns' 45-yard line. A pass completion to Ray Renfro took them to the Giants' 41, but a 19-yard sack dropped Cleveland back to its own 40. One last completion took them back to Giants territory, and Groza came on to try a 55-yard field goal with 25 seconds left. It fell well short. Because of Summerall's unlikely clutch kick, the teams were tied for first and would meet in a playoff one week later to determine the Eastern champion.

Pat Summerall

Alex Webster would kid Pat Summerall that if Alex had held onto that third-down touchdown pass, Pat never would have had the chance to be a hero and no one would have ever heard of him. As it turned out, though, Summerall's kick is one of the greatest moments in team history, and it capped his first season in New York.

Summerall was a fourth-round draft pick of the Lions in 1952. He was on the roster of the NFL champions that year but only got into two games as an end. Traded to the Cardinals the following season, Summerall began the kicking career for which he is remembered. In five seasons with the hapless Cardinals, Pat never made 50 percent of his field goals. His fortunes changed in 1958, when the Giants traded Dick Nolan and a No. 1 pick to the Cardinals to obtain Summerall and Lindon Crow.

Summerall found a whole different atmosphere in New York. Center Ray Wietecha's snaps were sharp and accurate, while holder Charley Conerly's soft hands provided Summerall with a dependable spot throughout his four years as a Giants player. Coached by Tom Landry, Summerall became one of the best kickers in football.

After three title games in four seasons, Summerall retired at age 31 to go into radio and television. His smooth, vocal delivery afforded Pat a 45-year career in the booth. He not only broadcast football, but also annual major events in golf and tennis. He was known for his intelligent, minimalist, low-key style, which highlighted the game itself and gave his colorful analyst partners, Tom Brookshier and John Madden, room to shine. Late in life, Summerall achieved perhaps his most heroic act of all by confronting his alcoholism and changing his life.

> **I** couldn't believe Jim Lee was asking me to do that. That was the longest attempt I'd ever made for the Giants. It was a bad field and so unrealistic. Most of the fellows on the bench couldn't believe it either. They wanted another pass play.
>
> —PAT SUMMERALL, IN *THERE WERE GIANTS IN THOSE DAYS* BY GERALD ESKENAZI

Pat Summerall scored 563 points during his NFL career.

January 20, 1991

Taking the Heart from San Francisco

Giants Win NFC on Final Play

The Giants and the 49ers stormed through the 1990 season on a collision course for a *Monday Night Football* showdown in San Francisco in Week 12. Both teams won their first 10 games and then lost in Week 11 before the most anticipated game of the year.

In the prime-time, hard-fought defensive battle, the two-time defending champion 49ers survived, 7–3, despite the Giants twice having a first-and-goal—New York could only manage a field goal in those eight plays. Both teams would lose just one more game before the playoffs, but New York suffered an even bigger loss against the Buffalo Bills: starting quarterback Phil Simms went down to a season-ending foot injury. The team's fortunes fell into the hands of career backup Jeff Hostetler and the rugged Giants defense.

The first half set the fierce tone for the NFC Championship Game. The 49ers took the opening kickoff and drove far enough for a field goal. The Giants answered with a 15-play drive for their own field goal. These were the two best defenses in the league, and the hitting was ferocious right from the start. Defenders on both sides were delivering shots that left bodies strewn on the field. The second quarter saw two more field goals and a 6–6 tie at the half.

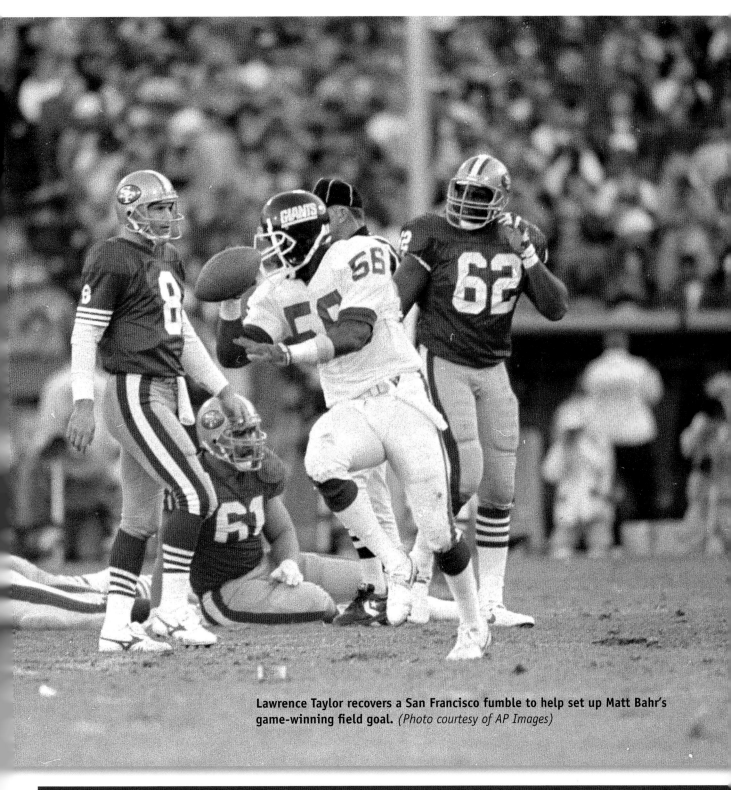

Lawrence Taylor recovers a San Francisco fumble to help set up Matt Bahr's game-winning field goal. *(Photo courtesy of AP Images)*

Game Details

New York Giants 15 • San Francisco 49ers 13

Giants	3	3	3	6	**15**
49ers	3	3	7	0	**13**

Date: January 20, 1991
Team Records: Giants 13–3, 49ers 14–2
Scoring Plays:
SF Cofer 47-yard FG
NYG Bahr 28-yard FG
NYG Bahr 42-yard FG
SF Cofer 35-yard FG
SF Taylor 61-yard pass from Montana (Cofer PAT)
NYG Bahr 46-yard FG
NYG Bahr 38-yard FG
NYG Bahr 42-yard FG

Early in the third quarter, Joe Montana hit John Taylor for a 61-yard scoring pass (which Everson Walls just missed intercepting) for the only touchdown in the game. The Giants continued with their game plan, though—a slow and steady ground game that would result in time-of-possession dominance of 39 to 21 minutes.

However, in the fourth quarter, New York still trailed 13–9. They needed some big plays, and soon. With less than 10 minutes to play, the 49ers faced third down at their own 23-yard line when Joe Montana rolled right to pass. Giants end Leonard Marshall was blocked and knocked down, but he scrambled to his feet and chased after Montana. Marshall nearly ran right through the 49ers quarterback, sending the ball flying and knocking Montana out of the game.

San Francisco punted, but New York's ensuing drive stalled at its own 46. As the Giants lined up to punt on fourth-and-two, Bill Parcells gave blocking back Gary Reasons a green light for a fake if he saw a hole. Reasons saw daylight, took the snap, and rumbled 30 yards to the 49ers' 16. Four plays later, Matt Bahr kicked his fourth field goal, and the Giants trailed by just a point with under six minutes to go.

With Steve Young now at quarterback, San Francisco tried to run out the clock. Roger Craig fumbled on the first play, but the 49ers recovered. Young then hit Brent Jones for 25 yards. After a couple more runs, the 49ers had a first down on the Giants' 30. On the next play, Roger Craig took the handoff as Giants tackle Eric Howard dropped to one knee to knife past guard Guy McIntyre and blast the ball out of Craig's grasp. Craig immediately swung around to grab it, but in that instant Lawrence Taylor popped up and snatched the ball out of the air.

The Giants had the ball at their own 43 with 2:36 left. Hostetler hit Mark Bavaro for 19 yards and Stephen Baker for 13 in a seven-play drive to the 49ers' 24, where Matt Bahr hit his fifth field goal as time expired. Giants 15, 49ers 13. There would be no three-peat for San Francisco; New York was headed for the Super Bowl to face the Buffalo Bills.

Leonard Marshall

The remarkable sequence of big plays in the last eight minutes of this championship game was started by Giants defensive end Leonard Marshall, who got up off his knees to run down Joe Montana and send both the quarterback and the ball flying. Marshall made a habit of making big plays during his 10-year career with the Giants. He was a complete player, strong against both the pass and the run.

A second-round draft pick out of LSU in 1983, Marshall was called "the steal of the draft" by the Raiders' Al Davis. It did not look that way at first. Marshall reported to training camp 20 pounds overweight and out of shape, with little pass-rushing technique. The Giants even assigned an assistant trainer to trail Marshall in the evenings and prevent him from making any late-night fast-food runs. Marshall worked hard, however, and within two years, Bill Parcells referred to him as one of the best "weight-room guys" on the team and cited that as the reason for his improvement as a player.

Leonard Marshall separates Joe Montana from the football and ends the quarterback's day to start the Giants' fourth-quarter comeback in the 1990 NFC Championship Game.

December 15, 1963

Giants Scrap Steelers 33–17 for Eastern Title

Giff's Single-Handed Scoop Is Decisive

Coach Buddy Parker had built the roughhouse Pittsburgh Steelers by trading draft choices for veterans, and they came into this game against the Giants with an odd record of 7–3–3. However, because ties did not count in the standings at the time, a victory over the 10–3 Giants would give Pittsburgh the crown by virtue of a slightly higher winning percentage.

On a frozen home field in windy, 25-degree conditions, the Giants came out fast and ran up a 16–0 lead—on a field goal by Don Chandler, a 41-yard bomb from Y. A. Tittle to Del Shofner, and a three-yard lob to Joe Morrison. Chandler missed the first extra point, but all Pittsburgh could manage in the first half was a field goal, leaving them trailing 16–3 at the intermission.

Finally, though, Pittsburgh appeared to be rolling in the third quarter. They scored quickly on a touchdown pass to Gary Ballman and had the Giants in a third-and-eight hole at the New York 24-yard line. Both coaches later cited the Giants' conversion of this vital third down as the turning point of the game because of the spectacular way it was accomplished.

Flanker Frank Gifford had been running sideline patterns against corner Glenn Glass throughout the contest. At this key moment of the game, Y. A. Tittle called a wing zig-in play. Gifford faked running another out and instead headed across the middle of

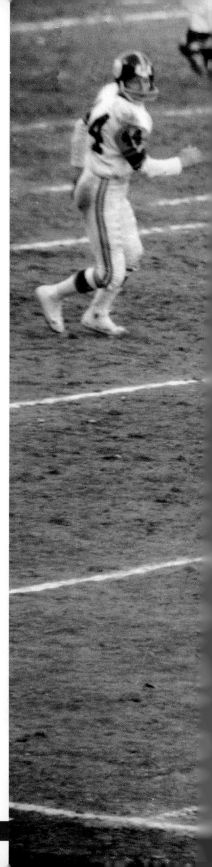

Although it wasn't quite as spectacular as his one-handed scoop catch in the same game, Frank Gifford catches a pass in front of Dick Haley (27) in the Eastern Conference clincher against the Steelers on the final day of the 1963 season. Note that both teams are wearing sneakers on the frozen field. *(Photo courtesy of AP Images)*

Don Chandler

With the final field goal in this game, Don Chandler became just the third Giants player to lead the league in scoring (after Ken Strong in 1934 and Choo Choo Roberts in 1949). No Giants player has managed the feat since. The 1963 season was Chandler's second as a place-kicker, but his eighth as the team's punter, and he performed both jobs well.

Chandler was a triple-threat back at the University of Florida who was drafted by the Giants in the fifth round in 1956 and converted into a punting specialist. Chandler had initial doubts about professional football, and he left camp before being intercepted at the airport by an enraged Vince Lombardi, who brought him back. Chandler rewarded that faith by leading the NFL in punting in 1957; Dave Jennings and Sean Landeta are the only other Giants punters to lead the league. When Pat Summerall retired in 1962, Chandler took over the place-kicking duties as well. After scoring more than 100 points in his first two years as a kicker, Chandler had an off year in 1964, and Allie Sherman traded him to Vince Lombardi's Packers for a third-round pick, which the Giants used on Bob Timberlake.

While Timberlake was hitting just one of 15 field-goal attempts and then vanishing from the league, Chandler joined Green Bay in time for its late 1960s three-peat. He kicked the controversial 1965 playoff field goal against the Colts that led to the uprights being raised 20 feet the following year. Two years later he scored 15 points in his final game, Super Bowl II. Chandler played in nine title games in 12 seasons and won four championship rings, including ones in both his first and last seasons.

Kicker Don Chandler led the NFL in scoring in 1963—no Giants player has done so since.

the field, leaving Glass going in the wrong direction. Tittle's pass was low, but Gifford bent over and scooped it up at his knees with just one hand and scurried upfield. Glass caught up to Gifford at the Pittsburgh 47 and tackled him after a 29-yard gain. Tittle went back to Gifford on the next play for 25 yards. He then shot a short pass to fullback Joe Morrison, who ran down the sideline for a 22-yard touchdown.

Three minutes later, Morrison scored his second touchdown of the day on a short plunge, and New York had a commanding 30–10 lead. Pittsburgh added another touchdown on a bomb to Buddy Dial, and Chandler would close out the scoring in the final period with a field goal that gave him the NFL scoring title.

Game Details

New York Giants 33 • Pittsburgh Steelers 17

Steelers	0	3	14	0	**17**
Giants	9	7	14	3	**33**

Date: December 15, 1963
Team Records: Giants 10–3, Steelers 7–3–3
Scoring Plays:
NYG Chandler 34-yard FG
NYG Shofner 41-yard pass from Tittle (Chandler kick failed)
NYG Morrison 3-yard pass from Tittle (Chandler PAT)
PIT Michaels 27-yard FG
PIT Ballman 21-yard pass from Brown (Michaels PAT)
NYG Morrison 22-yard pass from Tittle (Chandler PAT)
NYG Morrision 1-yard run (Chandler PAT)
PIT Dial 40-yard pass from Brown (Michaels PAT)
NYG Chandler 41-yard FG

On the Offensive

October 30, 2005

Well Done, Mr. Barber

Giants Rip Redskins in Tribute to Mara

Tiki Barber was at Wellington Mara's bedside to say good-bye to the dying team owner on the Monday before this game. Barber, like so many Giants players over the years, had grown close to Mara, and was distressed at his death on Tuesday.

Barber led his teammates into a packed St. Patrick's Cathedral on Friday for the emotional funeral services, which were attended by many former players as well as such former coaches as Bill Parcells, Bill Belichick, John Fox, Romeo Crennell, and Charlie Weis. All returned to honor the memory of a great man who touched many lives in and out of football. On Sunday, though, there was still a game against traditional rival Washington at Giants Stadium, and New York was ready.

The most important play of this game was the very first one from scrimmage: Tiki Barber took a handoff from Eli Manning, slipped around the left end, and sprinted down the sideline for 57 yards. Barber's initial burst set the dominating tone for the game, and it would not be his last. That first run led to a field goal, and the Giants added a second three-pointer later in the quarter to go up 6–0.

Early in the second quarter, Barber cut back to the left again and raced 59 yards before he was dragged down from behind at the 1-yard line. Two plays later, Brandon Jacobs powered in for the touchdown and the rout was on. New York added two more field goals in the period and went into halftime with a 19–0 lead, having outgained Washington 261 yards to 34 in the first half.

Jeremy Shockey caught a touchdown pass to open the third quarter and Jay Feely added a fifth field goal to increase the lead to 29–0, but there was one more

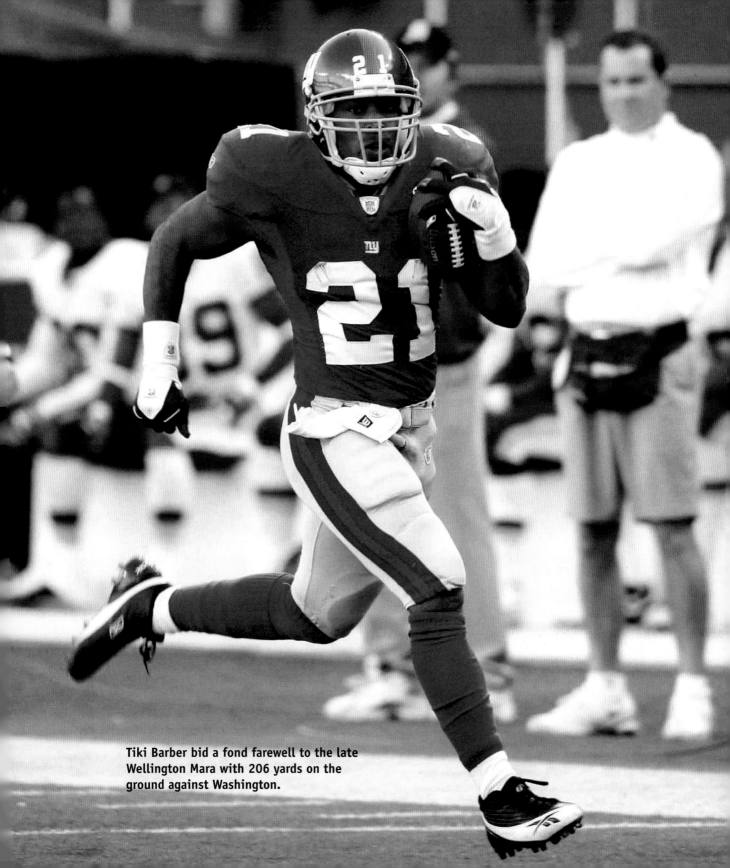

Tiki Barber bid a fond farewell to the late
Wellington Mara with 206 yards on the
ground against Washington.

piece of unfinished business to make the day perfect. From the Redskins' 4, Barber took the handoff and scampered into the end zone for his own six-point tribute to Mara. Barber had promised Mara's grandson Tim McDonnell, who for many years worked as a ballboy in Giants training camps, that he would score a touchdown for his grandfather. Barber tossed the ball to McDonnell when he got back to the sideline.

In the locker room after this 36–0 victory, Eli Manning presented the game ball to Wellington's son and heir, John. The Giants had outgained the Redskins 386 yards to 125, and had gained 262 yards on the ground—206 of them from Barber. It was a game that old Wellington would have loved.

Game Details

New York Giants 36 • Washington Redskins 0

Redskins	0	0	0	0	**0**
Giants	6	13	17	0	**36**

Date: October 30, 2005

Team Records: Giants 4–2, Redskins 4–2

Scoring Plays:

NYG Feely 39-yard FG
NYG Feely 50-yard FG
NYG Jacobs 3-yard run (Feely PAT)
NYG Feely 33-yard FG
NYG Feely 39-yard FG
NYG Shockey 10-yard pass from Manning (Feely PAT)
NYG Feely 44-yard FG
NYG Barber 4-yard run (Feely PAT)

TIKI'S take

This first game after Wellington Mara's death was an emotional one for me and my teammates. We took it to the Redskins right from the start, with me breaking free for a 57-yard run on the game's first play, though I was stopped before I could reach the end zone. In the second quarter, I broke another long run of 59 yards, but was dragged down from behind at the 1-yard line. One of Mr. Mara's 40 grandchildren, Tim McDonnell, was a former Giants ballboy who was on the sideline that day and he began to tease me about not being able to reach the end zone. I promised him a touchdown for his grandfather before the game was over. Finally, I was able to power in from the 4-yard line in the third quarter. I took the ball right over to Tim and told him, "This one's for you. This one's for your grandpa."

Wellington Mara

Wellington Mara spent his whole life with the Giants. Once his father bought the franchise in 1925, when Wellington was nine, it became the family business destined to be passed down to the sons. Wellington got his nickname, "Duke," from the players, and the official NFL ball was christened Duke in his honor in 1941.

Wellington scouted college players for the Giants and ran the personnel side of the team, while his older brother Jack ran the financial side. In the mid-1960s, though, the system developed cracks. Wellington allowed the team to get old, and his brother Jack died, leaving him with added responsibilities. The team suffered, and so did Wellington's popularity with players, fans, and ultimately with Jack's son Tim, who owned the other 50 percent of the Giants. The Maras' bitter feud contributed to the team's decline on the field.

Once George Young turned the team around on the field, Wellington began to be viewed as one of the patriarchs of the league again. Indeed, his league-first attitude had been instrumental in assuring such necessary developments as revenue sharing and the merger with the AFL.

At Super Bowl XXI, team leader Harry Carson delighted in throwing his beloved boss in the shower to share in the celebration of the long-awaited championship. That was one of six titles the Giants won in Mara's life. For his lifelong contributions to pro football, Wellington was elected to the Hall of Fame in 1997, where he joined his deceased father, Tim Mara.

The passing of owner Wellington Mara in 2005 was mourned by millions of Giants fans. *(Photo courtesy of AP Images)*

November 8, 1970

Tarkenton's Late Comeback Clips Cowboys

Johnson Scores Twice to Top Dallas

After losing the first three games of the 1970 season, the Giants got on a roll and won the next four to post a winning record for the first half of the year. One of the losses was to the Cowboys, a perennial power who came into Yankee Stadium on November 8 bearing a 5–2 record, tied for first with the Cardinals.

The first half of the game went pretty much as expected, with the Cowboys taking a 17–6 lead on two bombs from Craig Morton to Bob Hayes, one for 38 yards and the other for 80. All the Giants could manage were two Pete Gogolak field goals, and Gogolak missed a 55-yard try shortly before halftime. However, New York got a lift at the end of the half when they moved to the Dallas 47-yard line with 16 seconds left. This time, Gogolak was true, making a 54-yard kick to draw the Giants three points closer.

Dallas extended its lead to 20–9 with a field goal in the third quarter, but the Giants responded with a 71-yard drive on which star runner Ron Johnson carried the ball on seven of the 10 plays for 54 yards, including the last four for the score. The Giants recovered the

Acquired from the Vikings in 1967, quarterback Fran Tarkenton brought spirit and steadiness to a struggling New York franchise.

Ron Johnson

This stirring comeback win over the Cowboys was achieved largely because of the multidimensional skill set of running back Ron Johnson, who ran for 140 yards and caught four passes—including the game-winner—for 59 more yards. Johnson and Fran Tarkenton meshed perfectly in 1970 and gave the undermanned Giants a real chance to win each week.

Johnson was the first-round draft choice of the Browns in 1969, but they were disenchanted with his rookie season; they also needed a wide receiver to replace Paul Warfield, whom they had traded. So Johnson and two other Browns were packaged to the Giants for end Homer Jones. Johnson became the first Giants runner to exceed 1,000 yards rushing in a season in 1970, and he duplicated that feat in 1972. In fact, the only two winning seasons for the Giants from 1964 to 1981 were the two years that Johnson ran for 1,000 yards. He was a fast, elusive, slashing runner, a dependable receiver out of the backfield, and the workhorse centerpiece of New York's offense.

Unfortunately, Johnson needed knee surgery in 1971 and missed most of that season. In 1973, he played through a host of injuries and was not himself, although he did gain more than 900 yards. By 1974, he was a worn-down shadow of the player he had been. He retired after the 1975 season, second only to Alex Webster in career rushing yards for the Giants. He later achieved great success as a local businessman.

Running back Ron Johnson scored twice in a 1970 victory over the Dallas Cowboys. (Photo courtesy of WireImages)

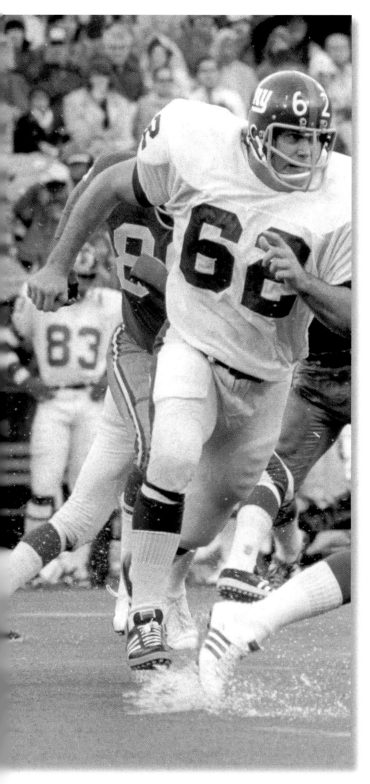

Game Details

New York Giants 23 • Dallas Cowboys 20

Cowboys	10	7	3	0	**20**
Giants	3	6	7	7	**23**

Date: November 8, 1970
Team Records: Giants 4–3, Cowboys 5–2
Scoring Plays:
DAL Clark 28-yard FG
NYG Gogolak 40-yard FG
DAL Hayes 38-yard pass from Morton (Clark PAT)
NYG Gogolak 42-yard FG
DAL Hayes 80-yard pass from Morton (Clark PAT)
NYG Gogolak 54-yard FG
DAL Clark 22-yard FG
NYG Johnson 4-yard run (Gogolak PAT)
NYG Johnson 13-yard pass from Tarkenton (Gogolak PAT)

ensuing surprise onside kick, and Johnson carried the ball five more times to get them into field-goal range. But Gogolak missed the 29-yard chip shot.

The Giants were still trailing 20–16 when they got the ball in the final minutes of the game. Fran Tarkenton completed passes to Johnson and Clifton McNeil—who was playing with a broken nose—to move the ball to the 17. A scramble got four yards and left New York facing a third-and-six.

On the game-winning play, Tarkenton sent Johnson circling out of the backfield. Ron was picked up by All-Pro cornerback Mel Renfro, but he beat Renfro to the goal post, where Tarkenton hit him for the touchdown with three minutes remaining. Dallas had plenty of time to come back, but the Giants defense rose up and stopped the Cowboys on downs to preserve the win.

Leading the late comeback against Philadelphia in 2006 was a major step in the maturation of quarterback Eli Manning.

Eli's Coming Back

Manning Hits Burress in Overtime to Ground Eagles

One never knows what strange things to expect from an Eagles-Giants game, and this one was as unpredictable as could be. After the Giants took the opening kickoff and drove right down the field to score on a touchdown pass to Amani Toomer, the lights went out for New York. The Eagles scored the next 24 points over the first three quarters and led 24–7 going into the fourth. Philadelphia had outgained the Giants 406 yards to 108, and Donovan McNabb had outpassed Eli Manning 320 yards to 146. Manning had been sacked six times, and Eagles-killer Tiki Barber had just 14 yards on 10 carries.

It all changed in the most improbable fashion: the Giants started their magnificent road comeback by fumbling. As the fourth quarter started, the Giants had reached their own 45-yard line, having started the drive at their own 9 four minutes before. A run and a pass gave New York a first down on the Eagles' 39. Manning dropped back again and hit Plaxico Burress over the middle. As Burress was being tackled, Brian Dawkins stripped the ball at the 16. Eagles safety Michael Lewis tried to fall on the ball at the 5, but it bounced into the end zone, where the Giants' Tim Carter recovered it for an incredible touchdown.

But even with this good fortune, time was running out. Neither the Eagles nor the Giants could move the ball the next two times they had it, and the Eagles started to run out the clock. However, Eagles star Brian Westbrook fumbled at his own 32, and the Giants recovered the ball with 4:11 to play. Four plays later, Manning hit Amani Toomer for a 22-yard touchdown, and New York trailed by only three with 3:28 to go.

Philadelphia managed just one first down and then punted back to the Giants, who took over on their own 20 with no timeouts and 58 seconds left. New York moved to midfield with 15 seconds to go. Manning then hit Jeremy Shockey at the Eagles' 32, and Eagles defensive

Plaxico Burress catches the 31-yard game-winning touchdown pass ahead of reaching Eagles cornerback Sheldon Brown. *(Photo courtesy of AP Images)*

Eli Manning

Every time Eli Manning gave a great performance, football pundits would speculate about whether it signaled a new level of his maturation or was merely an exceptional game that again indicated his immense potential. In his first four years, Manning exhibited a strong penchant for inconsistency not uncommon for young quarterbacks, but as his days of youthful inexperience dwindled, his tendency to mix great throws with awful misses or confounding interceptions began to look like the real Eli.

Eli Manning, of course, followed his famous father Archie (No. 2 overall draft pick in 1971) and brother Peyton (No. 1 overall draft pick in 1998) as the No. 1 overall draft choice of San Diego in 2004. Except, à la John Elway in 1983, he announced before the draft that he would never play for the Chargers, and thus forced a trade to the Giants who coveted him. The Giants gave up their 2004 No. 1 pick (quarterback Philip Rivers) as well as another No. 1 pick, plus a third and a fifth, for Manning's rights. Before Super Bowl XLII, Giants fans wondered whether he was worth the high price.

From season to season, there was incremental improvement in Manning's completion percentage and passer rating, but the maddening inconsistency of both quarterback and team continued. While his arm and ability were unquestioned, his quiet demeanor and somewhat lethargic personality bred doubt as to his eventual success. Before he died, quarterback guru Bill Walsh said that it was time for Eli to stop being Peyton's little brother and become the Giants' quarterback. It was time in 2007. In his fifth year, Phil Simms made a quantum leap forward and spent the next decade as a top NFL quarterback; Giants fans saw Manning make that leap in winning the title as Super Bowl MVP.

TIKI'S take

The funny thing about this game was that the Eagles' Trent Cole got called for a penalty after he tried to kick Kareem McKenzie in the groin, even though Kareem was just trying to help Cole get up. That penalty put the game-tying field-goal attempt into Jay Feely's range. Amani Toomer was phenomenal in this game, catching 12 passes for 137 yards while the rest of us were struggling. It was his consistency that kept us alive so that Eli could loft that game-winning touchdown to Plaxico Burress at the end. The Eagles were blitzing on the play and I missed my block on the linebacker, but Eli shot the ball high over cornerback Sheldon Brown where only Plaxico could grab it. It was such a brutally hot and humid day that when we finally won the game in overtime, none of us had the energy to celebrate. We were all too exhausted.

end Trent Cole was flagged 15 more yards for trying to kick Giants guard Kareem McKenzie. That loss of composure by Philadelphia allowed Jay Feely to kick his game-tying field goal from 35 yards away instead of 50. The game was sent into overtime.

While both teams were physically drained on this 79-degree day, the Eagles were shell-shocked as well. Neither team could score on its first possession, but New York began to move on its second chance. Twelve plays took the Giants from their own 15 to the Eagles' 31 and set the stage for the game-winning play. Facing a third-and-11, Manning realized an all-out blitz was coming and alerted Burress to look up fast.

Manning dropped back swiftly, but just as quickly blitzing safety Brian Dawkins was in his face. Eli tossed a high arcing pass to the 6'5" Burress over the head of Eagles cornerback Sheldon Brown; Burress caught it at the 5, carrying Brown into the end zone with him for the win. Burress jumped up and threw the ball into the stands while the normally stoic Manning leaped into the arms of guard Chris Snee to punctuate this thrilling Giants victory. Meanwhile, the thoroughly dehydrated Amani Toomer and Tim Carter had to be helped from the field and needed multiple IV bags in the locker room before they could truly savor this great win.

Game Details

New York Giants 30 • Philadelphia Eagles 24

Giants	7	0	0	17	6	**30**
Eagles	7	10	7	0	0	**24**

Date: September 17, 2006

Team Records: Giants 0–1, Eagles 1–0

Scoring Plays:

NYG Toomer 37-yard pass from Manning (Feely PAT)

PHL Westbrook 12-yard run (Akers PAT)

PHL Stallworth 20-yard pass from McNabb (Akers PAT)

PHL Akers 37-yard FG

PHL Brown 23-yard pass from McNabb (Akers PAT)

NYG Carter fumble recovery in end zone (Feely PAT)

NYG Toomer 22-yard pass from Manning (Feely PAT)

NYG Feely 35-yard FG

NYG Burress 31-yard pass from Manning

October 28, 1962

Triumphant Tittle Tosses Seven Touchdowns

Giants Bombard Redskins 49–34

The last bastion of the color line in the NFL fell in 1962 when Washington obtained their first black player, Hall of Fame receiver Bobby Mitchell. Just like that, a Redskins team that finished 1–12–1 in 1961 went into Yankee Stadium in Week 7 of the 1962 season undefeated and in first place at 4–0–2. The Giants trailed Washington with a 4–2 record and were expected to be slowed by two key injuries. First, Pro Bowl wide receiver Del Shofner had injured his shoulder in Week 5 against the Steelers, and he had played sparingly in Week 6 against the Lions. Second, ace quarterback Y. A. Tittle hurt his arm against Detroit and hadn't practiced all week. Knowing this, no one would have predicted what unfolded that day.

Tittle got off to a slow start, with six of his first seven passes falling incomplete. Things got worse after the Giants' Johnny Counts muffed a punt and Redskins quarterback Norm Snead hit Bobby Mitchell for a 44-yard score on the next play. After the ensuing kickoff, New York finally

Y. A. Tittle tosses one of his seven touchdown passes against the Redskins on October 28, 1962.

got a drive going despite two holding penalties, and Tittle hit Joe Morrison for a 22-yard touchdown to even the score.

The second quarter got underway with an interception of Snead by Erich Barnes. Tittle drove the Giants down the field on passes to Shofner, and then hit former Redskins tight end Joe Walton for a four-yard touchdown. Snead countered with another drive and touchdown pass, although Sam Huff blocked the extra point to retain a one-point New York lead. Another long pass to Shofner took the Giants to the Washington 4-yard line, and Tittle's two-yard pass to Joe Morrison right before the half was his third touchdown pass of the day.

On the first play of the second half, Snead got the Redskins back in the game with an 80-yard bomb to Mitchell, but the Giants took complete control of the game on the ensuing posession. Five straight Tittle completions culminated with a 32-yard touchdown to Shofner. Tittle's fifth touchdown pass went to Walton for 26 yards, and his sixth to Frank Gifford for 63 yards. The league record for touchdown passes in a game was seven, held by Sid Luckman and Adrian Burk, so that left Tittle just one shy. In the midst of this scoring explosion, Y. A. completed 12 passes in a row, just one short of another NFL record, as the Giants took a commanding 42–20 lead into the fourth quarter.

Midway through the final period, Tittle hit Shofner again for 50 yards to take the ball to the Washington 15. Three plays later came the record-tying seventh touchdown pass on a well-crafted play. With Walton and Gifford on the right side, the two ran crisscrossing patterns—Gifford in and Walton out—that confused Washington's secondary and left Walton all alone by the flag, where Tittle hit him for the last touchdown. The crowd began calling for touchdown pass No. 8, but Tittle took the air out of the ball with the Giants up by 29 points. The Redskins managed two late touchdowns to make the score closer, but Tittle did not counter with any further air strikes.

For the day, Shofner caught 11 passes for 269 yards, and Tittle completed 27-of-39 for 505 yards and those

Game Details

New York Giants 49 • Washington Redskins 34

Redskins	7	6	7	14	**34**
Giants	7	14	21	7	**49**

Date: October 28, 1962
Team Records: Giants 4–2, Redskins 4–0–2
Scoring Plays:
WSH Mitchell 44-yard pass from Snead (Khayat PAT)
NYG Morrison 22-yard pass from Tittle (Chandler PAT)
NYG Walton 4-yard pass from Tittle (Chandler PAT)
WSH Dugan 24-yard pass from Snead (Khayat kick blocked)
NYG Morrison 2-yard pass from Tittle (Chandler PAT)
WSH Mitchell 80-yard pass from Snead (Khayat PAT)
NYG Shofner 32-yard pass from Tittle (Chandler PAT)
NYG Walton 26-yard pass from Tittle (Chandler PAT)
NYG Gifford 63-yard pass from Tittle (Chandler PAT)
NYG Walton 6-yard pass from Tittle (Chandler PAT)
WSH Snead 1-yard run (Khayat PAT)
WSH Junker 35-yard pass from Snead (Khayat PAT)

> **I**t would have been in bad taste.
> —Y. A. TITTLE, IN RESPONSE TO CALLS FROM TEAMMATES AND FANS TO GO FOR EIGHT TOUCHDOWN PASSES

seven touchdowns—not bad for a couple of banged-up veterans. The Giants were within a game of first place; they would not lose again until the championship game against the Packers. By contrast, the upstart Redskins would lose seven of their last eight games and finish in fourth place in the East.

Del Shofner

Y. A. Tittle's roommate also came to the Giants in a 1961 trade, and he gave Tittle the best target he ever had. Del Shofner was a tall, wispy, injury-prone receiver who had great hands and blazing speed. He and Tittle teamed up to form the best long-ball threat in the game, as they showed on a 32-yard touchdown on this day of seven touchdown passes.

Shofner was originally drafted by the Rams with a No. 1 pick they had obtained from the Giants for Hall of Fame defensive end Andy Robustelli. Shofner first played defensive back but then was shifted to receiver, and he led the NFL in receiving yards in his second season.

After an injury-riddled 1960 season, Shofner was dealt to the Giants for a first-round draft pick. He led the Giants in receiving for the next three seasons, setting a club record in 1961 with 68 catches. He went over 1,000 yards each year from 1961 to 1963 and scored 32 touchdowns in that time, only missing one game to injury. Age and injuries caught up to him after 1963, though. In his last four seasons, he only played in 37 games and caught 54 passes for just three touchdowns. For his career, he averaged 18.5 yards per catch and was a five-time All-Pro.

Wide receiver Del Shofner teamed with Y. A. Tittle to form one of the game's most dangerous passing combinations. *(Photo courtesy of WireImages)*

Amani Toomer races past Marcus Coleman and Victor Green for an 80-yard touchdown in the Giants' 41–28 victory over the Jets.

Toomer Toasts the Tuna with Three Touchdowns

Giants Beat Jets 41–28

In many ways, this 1999 win over the Jets signaled a new beginning for the Giants under Jim Fassel. It was just the second start as a Giant for free-agent quarterback Kerry Collins, and on this day he would become the first Giants quarterback to exceed 300 yards passing since Phil Simms six years earlier. With Fassel mourning the death of his mother and the team mired at 5–6, it was the first chance for quarterbacks coach Sean Payton to call the plays and open up the offense.

On the other sideline, it would be the first time that former coach Bill Parcells returned to Giants Stadium as a visitor and lost. It would be the first and only time that injury-prone Giants runner Joe Montgomery gained more than 100 yards, and it would be the first time that the Giants would

Game Details

New York Giants 41 • New York Jets 28

Jets	0	7	0	21	**28**
Giants	17	10	7	7	**41**

Date: December 5, 1999

Team Records: Giants 5–6, Jets 4–7

Scoring Plays:

NYG Blanchard 41-yard FG

NYG Montgomery 4-yard run (Blanchard PAT)

NYG Toomer 61-yard pass from Collins (Blanchard PAT)

NYJ Johnson 13-yard pass from Lucas (Hall PAT)

NYG Collins 1-yard run (Blanchard PAT)

NYG Blanchard 31-yard FG

NYG Toomer 9-yard pass from Collins (Blanchard PAT)

NYJ Green 10-yard pass from Lucas (Hall PAT)

NYJ Chrebet 10-yard pass from Lucas (Hall PAT)

NYG Toomer 80-yard pass from Collins (Blanchard PAT)

NYJ Chrebet 5-yard pass from Lucas (Hall PAT)

Any time you can step on the field and have the opportunity to make things happen, you do it. I think today I just had the opportunity. The quarterback is making me look good. It's a combination of things when I have a game like this.

—AMANI TOOMER

boast a 300-yard passer, a 100-yard runner, and two 100-yard receivers in the same game.

The Giants got off to a fast start by scoring the first three times they got the ball in the first quarter—on a field goal, a run by Montgomery, and a 61-yard touchdown pass from Collins to Toomer. On the key touchdown pass, Collins and Toomer gave an indication that they were going to make a dangerous combination when they made a slight adjustment to the defensive coverage at the line. Toomer broke off his route and ran a quick slant. Collins hit him precisely on his right shoulder, allowing Toomer to spin away easily from corner Aaron Glenn and race upfield for the touchdown.

At the half, the Giants were up 27–7, and they added another touchdown pass to Toomer in the third quarter. The Jets managed a couple of fourth-quarter scores, but still trailed 34–21 with less than four minutes to go. Payton caught the attention of the offense by still going full throttle, with Collins throwing a jump-ball bomb to Toomer, who out-leaped Marcus Coleman for the ball and again strode for the end zone. Tiki Barber said after the game, "Here we are leading late in the game and Sean is [calling for] bombs. I was flabbergasted, but I was impressed."

Toomer had a breakout game, with six catches for 181 yards and three scores, while the other starting receiver, Ike Hilliard, caught six for 121 yards in an impressive aerial assault. The Giants would go on to lose three of their last four games and finish 7–9, but in 2000 they would go to the Super Bowl behind the passing of Collins, the receiving of Toomer and Hilliard, and the multi-dimensional skills of Barber.

Amani Toomer

At long last, this three-touchdown performance was Amani Toomer's coming-out party. Toomer was a second-round pick out of Michigan in 1996, but he spent his first three seasons as a punt returner who could not get on the field as a receiver. He showed big-play ability by returning three punts for scores—including two in his first six games—but was unreliable on offense because he did not run precise routes and seemed lackadaisical.

In his fourth season, Toomer finally won a starting job and was averaging four catches a game for the first 10 games of the season, then upped that to six catches a game once Kerry Collins took over. At 6'3" with deceptive, long-striding speed, Toomer began working to develop his natural talent, and he became a sure-handed deep threat opposite shifty possession receiver Ike Hilliard. With the passage of time and the coming of Plaxico Burress, Toomer smoothly made the transition from deep threat to smart veteran possession receiver. In both guises, he used his speed and size to be a willing and effective downfield blocker for the Giants' running game.

As a rookie, Toomer tore the anterior cruciate ligament in his right knee, and he tore the ACL in his left knee in 2006, at age 32. However, he returned in 2007 as Eli Manning's reliable third-down target. By the time Toomer left the Giants after the 2008 season, he was their all-time leader in receptions, receiving yards, receiving touchdowns, and 100-yard receiving games.

Amani Toomer outpaces linebacker Marvin Jones on his way to a 61-yard touchdown in the first quarter of Toomer's breakout game against the Jets. He would go on to set scores of Giants career receiving records. *(Photo courtesy of AP Images)*

January 14, 2001

Collins Connects with Comella and Collars Vikings

Giants Return to Super Bowl

With the 7–4 Giants having lost two games in a row, head coach Jim Fassel made his famous guarantee that New York was going to the playoffs, and the team caught fire, winning its last five games to clinch home-field advantage in the postseason with the best record in the NFC. By contrast, the deep passing attack of the Minnesota Vikings staked them to an 11–2 record before they came back to earth, losing the last three games of the season while giving up 104 points—35 per game. Still, the flawed Vikings were the heavy favorites when they came into Giants Stadium for the 2000 NFC Championship Game. The football world was in for a shock.

From his film study, Giants offensive coach Sean Payton was convinced that Minnesota's cornerbacks were a real weakness that could be exploited, so the Giants came out throwing. After returning the opening kickoff

to the 26-yard line, New York took just four plays to score: a 16-yard pass to Amani Toomer, a 10-yard pass to Toomer, a two-yard run, and then a 46-yard bomb from Kerry Collins to a wide-open Ike Hilliard for a 7–0 lead two minutes into the game. When Moe Williams of the Vikings fumbled the ensuing kickoff and the Giants' Lyle West recovered at the Vikings' 18, the Giants went for the quick strike to an unlikely target. It was the play of the day.

Greg Comella was a free-agent fullback who was known for his blocking prowess and for having decent hands. On the next play, Comella flared to the right flat to draw in linebacker Dwayne Rudd before running for the end zone. As he turned at the goal line, Collins's pass was upon him quickly, and he grabbed it at face level in self-defense, falling awkwardly backward on his left foot, out of bounds. New York had a two-touchdown lead 2:07 into the game, and they would not relent.

Bulky, blocking fullback Greg Comella falls clumsily backward after making an awkward grab of a Kerry Collins pass for the Giants' second score against the Vikings on January 14, 2001. *(Photo courtesy of AP Images)*

TIKI'S take

In 2000, Sean Payton became our offensive coordinator and my career began to take off because he began to use me as an all-purpose, Marshall Faulk–type back. He freed me up with misdirection plays and screens, and our offense that year could not be stopped when we were clicking. Still, no one respected us and no one gave us a chance against the high-flying Vikings. Former Giants stars Lawrence Taylor, Harry Carson, and O.J. Anderson were on the sideline as honorary captains to cheer us on that day. L.T. kept shouting for us to "keep it going" as we poured it on Minnesota. I was excited that my lead blocker and good friend, Greg Comella, got to have a moment in the spotlight for a change by scoring the second touchdown with a tough catch in the end zone. Greg and I trained together, and his intensity and dedication to finding our opponent's weakness was inspirational to me. We were headed to the Super Bowl for the first and only time in my career.

> I told Kerry after the game, 'I'm honored to play with you. I'm honored to have you as a quarterback.' He did a phenomenal job of turning his life around. It shows you can do some great things in life.
>
> —MICHAEL STRAHAN

Game Details

New York Giants 41 • Minnesota Vikings 0

Vikings	0	0	0	0	**0**
Giants	14	20	7	0	**41**

Date: January 14, 2001
Team Records: Giants 12–4, Vikings 11–5
Scoring Plays:
NYG Hilliard 46-yard pass from Collins (Daluiso PAT)
NYG Comella 18-yard pass from Collins (Daluiso PAT)
NYG Daluiso 21-yard FG
NYG Jurevicius 8-yard pass from Collins (Daluiso PAT)
NYG Daluiso 22-yard FG
NYG Hilliard 7-yard pass from Collins (Daluiso PAT)
NYG Toomer 7-yard pass from Collins (Daluiso PAT)

Minnesota's best scoring chance all day came midway through the first quarter, when Daunte Culpepper hit Cris Carter in the end zone, but cornerback Emmanuel McDaniel muscled the ball free for an interception and a touchback. A poor Vikings punt led to a Giants field goal on the first play of the second quarter, and New York would add three more scores in the period. After a 43-yard pass to Ron Dixon, Collins hit Joe Jurevicius for an eight-yard touchdown pass four minutes later. A 10-play, 62-yard drive five minutes after that culminated in another field goal. Finally, just 12 seconds before the half, Collins capped another long drive with a seven-yard touchdown pass to Hilliard for a 34–0 lead.

Jim Fassel

With a simple statement the day before Thanksgiving 2000, Jim Fassel defined the season for the Giants: "This is a poker game. I'm shoving my chips to the center of the table. I'm raising the ante. This team is going to the playoffs." That statement of assurance and purpose seemed to have a visceral effect on the team; the players became more focused and determined. This NFC Championship Game would punctuate those words and prove to be the high point of Fassel's tenure in New York.

Fassel's years as the Giants' coach were inconsistent and up-and-down; the team went 58–53–1. New York surprisingly made the playoffs in his first season, but they stumbled to mediocrity the next two seasons and Giants defensive players were openly dubious of Fassel's decisions. With his job in jeopardy, Fassel changed his own destiny by rescuing the career of troubled quarterback Kerry Collins. Fassel got the best out of Collins and the team made the Super Bowl in 2000, but then stumbled again in 2001. The 2002 season seemed to be a new start, but the awful playoff collapse to the 49ers that year carried over to 2003, when Fassel lost control of a team that finished 4–12—and lost his job as well.

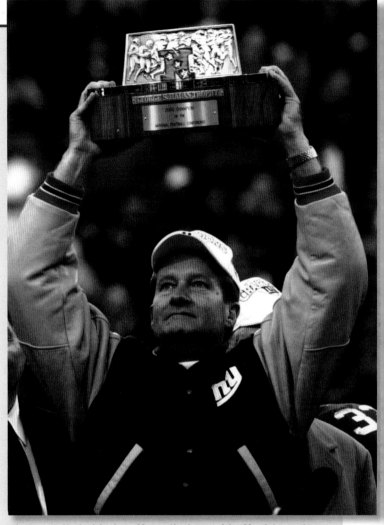

Jim Fassel's bold playoff prediction paid off with a trip to Super Bowl XXXV, the highpoint of his tenure with the Giants. *(Photo courtesy of AP Images)*

Minnesota's ever-so-slim hopes were erased on the very first play of the second half, when Giants safety Shaun Williams blitzed in and stripped Culpepper of the ball while he was sacking him. Cornelius Griffin recovered for New York at the 29, and five plays later Collins hit Amani Toomer for a seven-yard touchdown and the 41–0 final score.

It was a game of total domination on both sides of the ball for New York. Kerry Collins threw for 381 yards and five touchdowns; meanwhile, the sturdy Giants defense held the spectacular Vikings to 114 yards of total offense. The difference of 404 yards between Minnesota's total and the Giants' 518 was the largest disparity in the history of the NFL playoffs. For Minnesota, Cris Carter did not catch a pass until the fourth quarter, while Randy Moss caught just two passes for 18 yards. The Giants were going to the Super Bowl.

December 1, 1986

Rambo Rumbles Through San Francisco

Bavaro's 31-Yard Reception Keys Comeback Win over 49ers

Tied with the Redskins for first place in their division, the Giants rolled into San Francisco on a five-game winning streak for a *Monday Night Football* battle with the resurgent 49ers. This demanding and vital game would prove just how resilient and resourceful the 1986 Giants were on the road to the Super Bowl. However, it would take an extra-effort play by their sturdy tight end to spark them in the second half.

The 49ers dominated offensively and were up by 17–0 at the half on two touchdowns by Jerry Rice. Meanwhile, the ground attack of the ball-control Giants was being shut down by the stingy 49ers defense. For the game, the Giants would gain a paltry 13 yards rushing.

It was up to Phil Simms to shake things up with his arm. Ten minutes and 15 plays in the third quarter would prove crucial; the first play was the most decisive of all. The Giants first got the ball on the 49ers' 49-yard line, and Simms promptly hit tight end Mark Bavaro with a nine-yard pass over the middle. Two 49ers linebackers immediately tried to bring down Bavaro with arm tackles, but they slid right off him. Then Ronnie Lott jumped on Bavaro's back, but the tight end carried the fierce 49ers safety for a rough 17-yard ride as four other San Francisco defenders came in and hit Bavaro from the side, finally bringing him down at the 18.

Bavaro's astounding 31-yard reception got New York unstuck. Even though he later modestly attributed the gain to poor tackling, the dynamic catch-and-carry fired up the team. Three plays later, Simms slipped a short pass to Joe Morris, who went into the end zone from the 17 for the first Giants touchdown.

The next time the Giants got the ball, they started at their own 29. Four plays later, they faced a fourth-and-two at their own 49. Aggressively, New York went for it on fourth down; as Bill Parcells forcefully explained later, "I was trying to win the game." Simms handed the ball to Morris, who had thus far carried nine times for zero yards, and he ran around the weak-side end for a 17-yard pickup and a first down. On the next play, Simms hit Stacy Robinson for a

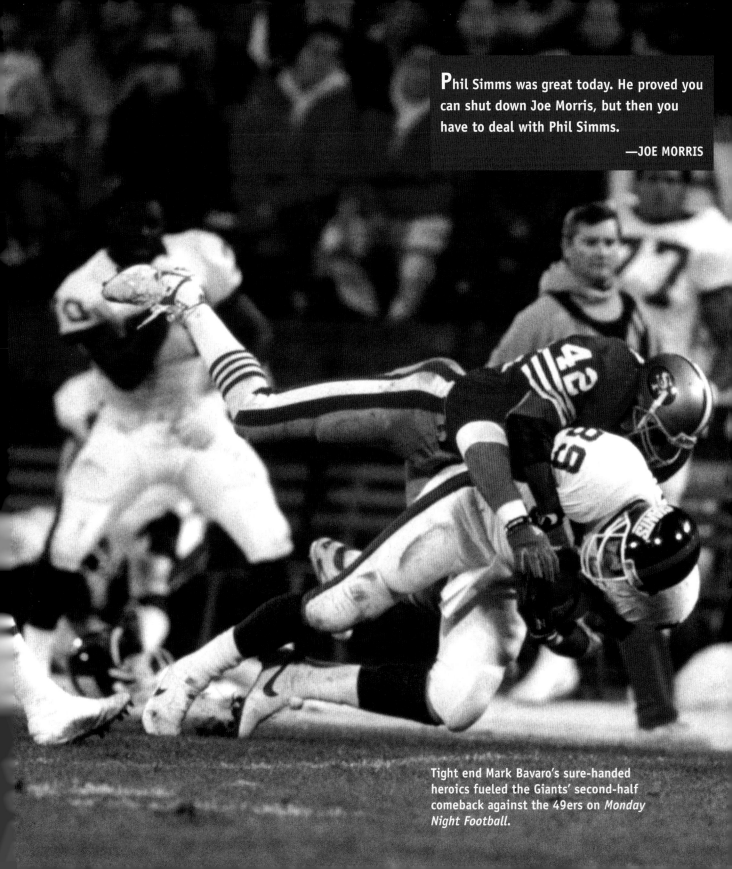

Phil Simms was great today. He proved you can shut down Joe Morris, but then you have to deal with Phil Simms.

—JOE MORRIS

Tight end Mark Bavaro's sure-handed heroics fueled the Giants' second-half comeback against the 49ers on *Monday Night Football*.

Joe Morris

Joe Morris's key 17-yard power burst on a fourth-and-two at midfield was typical of his reliability in the clutch. Bill Parcells liked to say of the undersized runner, "He's not small, he's short." Morris was 5'7" but was solidly built at 195 pounds. He had broken all the rushing records at Syracuse set by notable predecessors Jim Brown, Ernie Davis, Floyd Little, and Larry Csonka. The Giants picked him in the second round of the 1982 draft, but Morris found himself lodged behind first-round pick Butch Woolfolk. Morris finally began to earn playing time in 1984 as Woolfolk fell into disfavor, but then the Giants drafted George Adams with the 19th pick in 1985.

By then, though, Morris was ready to break out. He rushed for a team-record 1,336 yards and 21 touchdowns in 1985, and he exceeded 100 yards rushing in six different games as Adams faded from view. Both Parcells and offensive coordinator Ron Erhardt cited Morris's increased patience and improved ability to read his blocking as the factors that enabled Joe's great advance. Morris followed that season with 1,516 yards rushing and eight 100-yard games in the 1986 Super Bowl season. That record-setting season included back-to-back 181-yard games against the Redskins and the Cowboys in leading the Giants to the playoffs.

After those two great seasons, though, it was a quick downhill slide. Those two seasons were two of only three in his eight-year career in which he averaged more than four yards per carry. In 1985 and 1986, Morris gained more than half his career rushing yards and scored 70 percent of his touchdowns. In that time, though, he was arguably the best runner in the league and a giant on the field who keyed New York's ground attack.

Running back Joe Morris led the Giants in rushing during the 1985–1986 seasons.

Game Details

New York Giants 21 • San Francisco 49ers 17

Giants	0	0	21	0	**21**
49ers	3	14	0	0	**17**

Date: December 1, 1986
Team Records: Giants 10–2, 49ers 7–4–1
Scoring Plays:
SF Wersching 30-yard FG
SF Rice 11-yard pass from Montana (Wersching PAT)
SF Rice 1-yard run (Wersching PAT)
NYG Morris 17-yard pass from Simms (Allegre PAT)
NYG Robinson 34-yard pass from Simms (Allegre PAT)
NYG Anderson 1-yard run (Allegre PAT)

34-yard touchdown pass that Robinson let roll down to his legs before he secured the ball, and the Giants were within three points.

In short order, the Giants got the ball at their own 29 again. They moved the ball to midfield in three plays, and then Simms hit Robinson for a 49-yard bomb to the 1. From there, Ottis Anderson punched in the go-ahead touchdown with more than three minutes still left in the third quarter. Simms had completed eight of nine passes for 175 yards in the three rapid-fire Giants scoring drives.

In the final minutes, Montana began one of his patented comeback drives, leading the 49ers to the Giants' 17 with 1:16 left to play.

But on third-and-four, Wendell Tyler was stopped for a three-yard loss by Gary Reasons. He also fumbled the ball, but the play was allowed to stand. Then on fourth-and-seven from the 20, Montana was hit by linebacker Andy Headen as he tried to throw to Roger Craig over the middle, and the pass dropped harmlessly to the ground.

Shockey Stampedes the Colts

Giants Tight End Leads Team to Victory with Swagger

In a late-season drive for the playoffs, one wouldn't expect a rookie to lead the charge, but Jeremy Shockey was no ordinary rookie. The 8–6 Giants and the 9–5 Colts were desperately trying to stay afloat in 2002's tight playoff races as they came into this inter-conference battle in the next-to-last week of the season. One player who was ready for action was the aptly named Shockey, New York's flamboyant first-year tight end.

The Giants got onto the scoreboard first with a field goal following a blocked punt and then mounted a long drive later in the first quarter, after Dhani Jones intercepted a Peyton Manning pass at the Giants' 37-yard line. This drive and the New York offense were sparked by a screen pass to Shockey with the Giants facing a second-and-16 from the Colts' 38 on the first play of the second quarter. Shockey grabbed the pass and then began rumbling downfield. At the 25, Colts safety David Gibson, who had been widely quoted before the game describing Shockey as "just another player," got set to make the tackle.

Shockey saw Gibson, lowered his shoulder, and headed right for him. Shockey trampled over Gibson as if he were a Styrofoam cup and continued toward the end zone before the Colts finally lassoed him and brought him down at the 14. Shortly thereafter, Tiki Barber scored from the 4 and the Giants led by 10.

New York put the game away in the third quarter, starting with the first play from scrimmage. On a flea flicker, Barber took the handoff from Kerry Collins and flipped it

Jeremy Shockey steamrolled Colts safety David Gibson on his way to 116 receiving yards that quieted the boasts of the talkative Gibson, who had downplayed Shockey's impact before the game.

back to him, and Collins unleashed the bomb to Amani Toomer for an 82-yard touchdown with the victimized David Gibson in fruitless pursuit. The Giants scored two more touchdowns in the third period and went into the fourth quarter leading 30–6.

Collins added two more touchdown passes to Toomer in the final 15 minutes, while Peyton Manning led the Colts to three meaningless touchdowns to narrow the final score to 44–27. For the day, Kerry Collins achieved a perfect 158.3 passer rating and threw for 366 yards and four touchdowns. Toomer caught 10 passes for 204 yards and three scores, and Shockey caught seven for 116 yards. Although Shockey would also fumble inside the Colts' 10 on a later drive, his electric play inspired the entire team, and the Giants would go on to beat the Eagles in the last game of the season to make the playoffs as a wild card.

Game Details

New York Giants 44 • Indianapolis Colts 27

Giants	3	7	20	14	**44**
Colts	0	3	3	21	**27**

Date: December 22, 2002

Team Records: Giants 8–6, Colts 9–5

Scoring Plays:

NYG Bryant 20-yard FG

NYG Barber 4-yard run (Bryant PAT)

IND Vanderjagt 20-yard FG

NYG Toomer 82-yard pass from Collins (Bryant PAT)

NYG Stackhouse 18-yard pass from Collins (Bryant missed kick)

IND Vanderjagt 27-yard FG

NYG Barber 1-yard run (Bryant PAT)

IND Wayne 21-yard pass from Manning (run for two-point conversion failed)

NYG Toomer 21-yard pass from Collins (Bryant PAT)

IND Harrison 25-yard pass (Pollard two-point conversion pass from Manning)

IND Wayne 40-yard pass from Manning (Vanderjagt PAT)

NYG Toomer 27-yard pass from Collins (Bryant PAT)

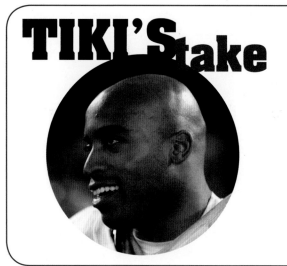

TIKI'Stake

When Jeremy Shockey joined the Giants in 2002, he shook up our team and gave us a jolt of energy. The all-out way he played the game made him a favorite of Giants fans and of Wellington Mara as well. Shockey was outspoken and outrageous and was the only teammate I had that called Mr. Mara by his nickname: "Duke." He was a great blocker and a terrific receiver who could be unstoppable when he got going, as Colts safety David Gibson found out on this play. I played a small motivational role in this play: Kerry Collins and I read Gibson's comments denigrating Shockey in the Indianapolis newspaper and made sure to pass them on to Jeremy that morning. You're welcome, David.

Jeremy Shockey

In a game in which veteran receiver Amani Toomer caught 10 passes for 204 yards and three touchdowns, the unforgettable moment was still Jeremy Shockey's first-quarter catch and run, in which he rumbled over safety David Gibson like an 18-wheeler mashing a rabbit on the highway.

Shockey went to the University of Miami, and in his second year there won a national title and was named All-American. He declared early for the 2002 NFL Draft, and the Giants grabbed him with the 14th pick in the first round. Jeremy made his presence known right away in training camp by sparking a fight in the dining hall about singing his school song. Surprisingly, coach Jim Fassel's reaction to the fight was, "My man has arrived," because he so loved Shockey's battling spirit.

His mouthiness wasn't always limited to opponents; after a loss to Seattle in 2006, he told the media "We got outplayed, and we got outcoached." Still, Shockey caught 66 passes and seven touchdowns in 2006 and 57 more passes in 2007. A season-ending injury kept Shockey out of the team's improbable Super Bowl XLII victory, and growing discontent between the Giants and their tight end eventually prompted New York to trade him to the Saints in 2008. He battled injuries during two up-and-down years in New Orleans, but bounced back to catch touchdown passes in the Saints' second-round playoff victory over the Arizona Cardinals and their Super Bowl XLIV victory over the Indianapolis Colts.

Tight end Jeremy Shockey brought plenty of swagger to the Giants as a rookie in 2002.

The double reverse didn't surprise me, but the lateral to Conerly? They couldn't have planned it. What the hell was he doing there?

—PAUL BROWN

The Giants' Charley Conerly, Alex Webster, and Frank Gifford completed a double hand-off and lateral to beat the Browns for the 1958 Eastern Division championship. *(Photo courtesy of AP Images)*

Hot-Potato Trick Play Beats Browns

First-Quarter Touchdown and Giants Defense Tops Cleveland

One week after beating Cleveland 13–10—on an improbable 49-yard field goal through the wind and snow—to tie for the Eastern Conference lead, the Giants and the Browns returned to Yankee Stadium for a playoff to determine the Eastern crown on an overcast 25-degree day. With a stalwart defense and a bit of surprising trickery on offense, New York took on a Browns team demoralized by the previous week's loss.

Cleveland coach Paul Brown tried to mix up his attack for this rematch. The previous week, he had called 37 runs, mostly by Jim Brown, and just 12 passes. In this game, he reversed that by calling 13 runs and 27 passes. Jim Brown was held to the lowest rushing total of his career, gaining a mere eight yards on just seven carries.

The Giants controlled the ball and the tempo from the start, getting off 71 plays to the Browns' 40. Both teams had trouble holding on to the ball; each had four turnovers. But the Giants kept their grip tight at just the right time.

In the first quarter, New York reached the Cleveland 19-yard line when Charley Conerly called a brand-new play the team had practiced all week. Conerly handed off to right halfback Alex Webster, who was heading left while guard Al Barry pulled to the right. Left halfback Frank Gifford slipped behind fullback Mel Triplett heading to the right and took a handoff from Webster on a reverse. Gifford cut upfield, between

Al Barry blocking Bob Gain on the outside and Dick Yelvington closing off Willie McClung on the inside. Gifford faked a lateral to get Gain to rise up and lean the wrong way as Gifford slid by. With linebacker Galen Fiss closing from the sideline and safety Ken Konz coming from the goal line, Gifford then lateraled the ball out to the sideline, where Conerly caught the ball at the 10. Gain and Konz were out of position, but safety Junior Wren hustled over to drill the 37-year-old Conerly as he dove into the end zone with what proved to be the only touchdown of the game.

Those are the only points the Giants would need on this inspired day, although Pat Summerall added a field goal in the second quarter for insurance. The closest Cleveland came to scoring was when they reached the Giants' 6 in the fourth quarter, but a Sam Huff interception ended that threat. The Browns would have the ball for only one out of the last 11 minutes of the game.

New York outgained Cleveland 211 to 24 on the ground and 317 to 86 in total yards, soundly beating their chief rival of the past decade. It was the first time Paul Brown's team had been shut out in 106 games; the last time had been when Giants coach Steve Owen opened his umbrella defense on Cleveland in October 1950. The Giants had earned their slot in the NFL title game against the Colts the next week in Yankee Stadium.

> **W**ell, I was supposed to be there. The lateral was an option. Vinnie [Lombardi] set it up that way. I was supposed to be there if Gifford needed me. I don't know how long it'd been since I scored a touchdown, but it was great for an old guy like me to run it in.
>
> —CHARLEY CONERLY, IN *GIANTS IN THEIR OWN WORDS*
> BY RICHARD WHITTINGHAM

Game Details

New York Giants 10 • Cleveland Browns 0

Browns	0	0	0	0	**0**
Giants	7	3	0	0	**10**

Date: December 21, 1958
Team Records: Giants 9–3, Browns 9–3
Scoring Plays:
NYG Conerly 10-yard lateral from Gifford after 8-yard run (Summerall PAT)
NYG Summerall 26-yard FG

Charley Conerly

Charley Conerly came through for the Giants countless times during the 14 seasons the taciturn Mississippian spent in New York. Conerly set a personal best for touchdowns and passing yards in his rookie season in 1948. However, he struggled for the next five years as coach Steve Owen switched back and forth between the T-formation and his own outdated A-formation.

In 1954, Vince Lombardi was hired to handle the offense, and Conerly's career turned around at age 33.

For the next eight seasons, under Lombardi and then Allie Sherman, Conerly enjoyed a golden era in which the team won and the fans were on his side at last. He was named league MVP in 1959 as he led the league in passing at age 38. When he retired at age 40 in 1961, only Otto Graham had won more quarterback starts than Charley's 77. Conerly also finished as the Giants' all-time leader with more than 19,000 yards passing and 173 touchdowns. His No. 42 jersey was retired by the team.

Sam Huff

Above all, Sam Huff had a sense of timing and drama. He came along at the right time in the right system, and he knew how to make the most of the opportunity. Tom Landry's 4-3 defense was designed to funnel plays to the middle linebacker, and Huff filled that role to the hilt. His furious battles with great runners like Jim Brown and Green Bay's Jim Taylor were rugged grudge matches that made all three deservedly famous.

Huff was a third-round draft pick in 1956 as a guard; he was shifted to linebacker in training camp. He won the starting job in his rookie year. Over his

> **N**ext time I give you the f*cking ball, you keep it.
>
> —CHARLEY CONERLY TO FRANK GIFFORD,
>
> IN *THE WHOLE TEN YARDS*

eight seasons in New York, Huff became a legend as the leader of the first defense to get the acclaim and cheers normally reserved for the offense. In 1959, he became the first NFL player ever to appear on the cover of *Time* magazine, and one year later he was the subject of a widely-seen CBS News documentary called "The Violent World of Sam Huff." The documentary was narrated by Walter Cronkite; it was the first time a player had been wired with a microphone for a game. Huff was a hard and sometimes late tackler who also had the speed to cover passes. He set a record for linebackers with 30 interceptions for his career.

Huff, along with many Giants fans, cried when he learned that Allie Sherman had traded him to Washington in 1964 as part of a youth movement. Huff got his revenge on Sherman in 1966, when he sent the Redskins' field-goal unit onto the field—without Washington coach Otto Graham's approval—to kick an insulting three-pointer in the closing seconds of a 72–41 pounding of the Giants. The five-time Pro Bowl player was elected to the Hall of Fame in 1982; he has broadcast Redskins games for more than 30 years.

Legendary linebacker Sam Huff was the foundation of Tom Landry's 4-3 defense.

January 9, 1994

Hampton Hies Away Home

Giants Vanquish Vikings 17–10 in Wild-Card Game

In Dan Reeves's first season as head coach, the Giants had the second-best record in the NFC on the strength of having the best defense in the NFL, allowing only 205 points. By losing the final game of 1993 to Dallas in overtime, however, New York found itself as a wild-card entry in the playoffs, playing host to a 9–7 Vikings team that gave up more points than it scored on the year. What seemed like a mismatch, though, turned out to be a dogfight on this windy 23-degree day with a minus-5-degree wind chill.

New York opened the scoring in the first quarter, on a 26-yard field goal with the wind. They lined up for a second field-goal try in the second quarter, but that kick into the wind was blown way off course. All the points in this game would be scored by the team that had the wind at its back.

Late in the second quarter, Minnesota took advantage of the wind and scored on a 40-yard pass from veteran Jim McMahon to Cris Carter with 1:53 left in the period. The Vikings forced a punt before the half and received a gift when punter Mike Horan's kick was blown into the shoulder of teammate Greg Jackson and traveled just 13 yards, to the Giants' 36-yard line. Two plays later, Fuad Reveiz kicked a 52-yard field goal on the final play of the first half, and the Giants went off the field trailing by a touchdown to a chorus of boos from the stands.

In the locker room, the players would get an earful from superstar Lawrence

Rodney Hampton stiff-armed his way to a 51-yard touchdown run against the Vikings in a playoff win on January 9, 1994.

Rodney Hampton

The 51-yard touchdown run by Rodney Hampton in this game showcased the power and speed of this remarkable Giants running back. It was the high point of a 161-yard rushing performance that carried the Giants past the Vikings in what would prove to be Hampton's last chance for a postseason win.

Hampton was a first-round draft pick in 1990, but unlike other first-round runners who flopped for New York such as Rocky Thompson, Butch Woolfolk, and George Adams, Hampton proved he was the real deal right from the start. As a rookie, he and Ottis Anderson were the team's lead ball carriers, but Hampton broke his leg in a playoff victory over the Bears and missed the Super Bowl run.

Under new coach Ray Handley, Hampton had his two best seasons, gaining more than 1,000 yards, averaging more than four yards per carry, and serving as a useful passing outlet. The next Giants coach, Dan Reeves, cast Hampton as a battering ram. He gained more than 1,000 yards three times but twice went over 300 carries, and averaged less than four yards a carry all four years.

Hampton was overworked under Reeves and began to break down physically with knee and back injuries. By the time Jim Fassel arrived in 1997, Hampton was a 28-year-old running back who had just 23 carries left in his career. His speed was gone and his power was diminished.

Hampton gained more than 1,000 yards in five consecutive seasons, and he played in two Pro Bowls. He retired as the all-time leading Giants rusher, having passed Joe Morris, although Tiki Barber was already on hand and would pass Hampton in the next decade.

Taylor and other veterans, imploring the team to step it up. Meanwhile, Reeves was making some alterations to a base play in the playbook that would change the momentum of the game.

On the fourth play of the second half, Phil Simms took the snap at the 49 and handed off to Rodney Hampton, who was sweeping to the right. Defensive tackle John Randle got a hand on Hampton in the backfield, but Hampton cut back behind Doug Riesenberg's block on Roy Barker. Linebacker Fred Strickland got a piece of Hampton at the Vikings' 47 but was pushed away by tight end Howard Cross. Hampton took off, with Chris Doleman and Carlos Jenkins in pursuit. Hampton stiff-armed Jenkins to the ground at the 30 and picked up speed. Downfield, receiver Chris Calloway was shielding safety Vencie Glenn, but Glenn slipped by Calloway at the 5—only to run face-first into another Hampton stiff-arm. Rodney went over him to complete a dominating 51-yard touchdown, which tied the game with 12:06 left in the third quarter.

Game Details

New York Giants 17 • Minnesota Vikings 10

Vikings	0	10	0	0	**10**
Giants	3	0	14	0	**17**

Date: January 9, 1994

Team Records: Giants 11–5, Vikings 9–7

Scoring Plays:

NYG Treadwell 26-yard FG

MIN Carter 40-yard pass from McMahon (Reveiz PAT)

MIN Reveiz 52-yard FG

NYG Hampton 51-yard run (Treadwell PAT)

NYG Hampton 2-yard run (Treadwell PAT)

A few minutes later a shanked Vikings punt gave New York the ball on the Minnesota 26. Eight plays after that, Hampton powered in from the 2 to put the Giants up 17–10 with 5:37 left in the third period. The extra-point snap was high, but kicker David Treadwell hoofed it into the end zone, pulling a calf muscle in the process. With the way the Giants were playing on defense, though, they would need no more points.

Rodney Hampton carried 33 times for 161 yards on the day, while Phil Simms could only manage 94 yards passing on what he ranked as one of the three worst weather days he ever experienced. It was the last home game and last win for both Simms and Lawrence Taylor. By contrast, it was the first playoff win for rookie stars Michael Strahan and Jesse Armstead. The next week, Simms's and Taylor's careers would end with a loss in San Francisco, but New York was raising a new crop of leaders.

Head coach Dan Reeves's halftime adjustments helped lead the Giants to playoff victory. *(Photo courtesy of WireImages)*

Tiki Barber heads upfield for a 95-yard touchdown run, the longest run from scrimmage in Giants history, on the road against the Raiders in 2005.

December 31, 2005

Barber Bursts 95 Yards to Playoffs

Giants Pound Raiders 30–21

While the Giants had already clinched a spot in the 2005 playoffs as they entered the season finale, they needed a victory in Oakland to win the division title and possibly secure a first-round bye. To add to the challenge, the 4–11 Raiders were led by former Giants quarterback Kerry Collins, who had extra motivation against his old club. To make matters worse, New York's defense was banged-up, and it featured three linebackers who had just been signed in the past week. In the face of these adversities, Giants MVP Tiki Barber loaded the team on his back and hauled them into the postseason.

The key play in this lackluster game—played in a half-empty stadium—came halfway through the first quarter. The Giants faced a second-and-14 from their own 5-yard line. Barber took the handoff from Eli Manning and slid

TIKI'S take

With us backed up at our own 5-yard line, we came out in a power running formation with fullback Jim Finn lined up on the strong side. The Raiders knew a strong-side run was the call and brought up both safeties to try to shut down the play. Finn's job was to block the strong-side linebacker, and when guard David Diehl pulled to lead the play, both the weak-side and middle linebackers followed him in that direction. With all of this defensive shifting, the middle of the field was left completely empty, and I cut right up the middle between guard Chris Snee and center Shaun O'Hara. Immediately, I avoided Stuart Schweigert and slid to the sideline accompanied by Plaxico Burress. Plax took care of cornerback Nnamdi Asomugha, the last Raider with a shot at me, and I sprinted 95 yards untouched on the longest scoring run in team history.

Game Details

New York Giants 30 • Oakland Raiders 21

Giants	7	13	7	3	**30**
Raiders	7	7	7	0	**21**

Date: December 31, 2005

Team Records: Giants 10–5, Raiders 4–11

Scoring Plays:

NYG Barber 95-yard run (Feely PAT)

OAK Moss 15-yard pass from Collins (Janikowski PAT)

NYG Feely 25-yard FG

NYG Burress 78-yard pass from Manning (Feely PAT)

NYG Feely 38-yard FG

OAK Gabriel 8-yard pass from Collins (Janikowski PAT)

NYG Jacobs 1-yard run (Feely PAT)

OAK Moss 44-yard pass from Collins (Janikowski PAT)

NYG Feely 46-yard FG

through a hole between center Shaun O'Hara and guard Chris Snee. A quick juke faked out Raiders safety Stuart Schweigert, who dove and missed Barber as Tiki made a sharp cut to the left and headed up the sideline, Amani Toomer and Plaxico Burress in front of him for interference. Tiki went 95 yards untouched to the end zone for the first touchdown of the game. In the process, he broke a 75-year-old team record formerly held by Hap Moran, who had raced 91 yards against the Packers in 1930 (although Moran was tackled at the 1 and did not score).

Big plays kept the Giants ahead throughout the game. With the score 10–7 in the second quarter and New York at its own 22, Manning hit Burress at the 35 and Plaxico sprinted untouched for a 78-yard score. Early in the third quarter, Chad Morton returned a Raiders punt 57 yards to the Oakland 3, and Brandon Jacobs pounded the ball in from there to extend the lead to 27–14. While Randy Moss would catch a second touchdown pass after that, the outcome of the game was never seriously in doubt.

Barber ended up with 203 yards rushing for the game, making it the third time that year and the second consecutive game in which he surpassed 200 yards on the ground. He also broke Rodney Hampton's team record of

49 rushing touchdowns and ended up with a Giants-best 1,860 yards rushing for the season.

The Giants won the NFC East and secured home-field advantage but it would do no good. One week later, the Carolina Panthers came into the Meadowlands, shut down Barber, and shut out the Giants 23–0 in Eli Manning's inauspicious playoff debut.

He's been outstanding. He's played with great consistency. He's taken good care of the ball. He's an extremely durable guy.

—TOM COUGHLIN ON TIKI BARBER

Tiki Barber retired as both the leading rusher and leading receiver in Giants history.

The Best Offense

Is a

Good Defense

December 10, 1989

Frozen Out

Giants' Big Stop in the Snow Beats Broncos

After starting the 1989 season 8–1, the Giants hit a rough patch and dropped three of the next four games. Headed for a road game in Denver with Lawrence Taylor unlikely to play, New York's run for the playoffs was beginning to disintegrate. Moreover, at game time the temperature was 23 degrees with a 15-mph wind and heavy snow falling. It was a day for defense, and led by inside linebacker Gary Reasons's 14 tackles, the Giants delivered.

New York got the ball for the first time on its own 15-yard line. A slow, steady 15-play mix of runs and passes culminated eight minutes and 53 seconds later with an Ottis Anderson three-yard touchdown run at the outset of the second quarter. Five minutes later, the Giants got the ball again in great field position after Dave Meggett's 26-yard punt return put the ball on the Denver 36. However, a penalty and a sack left the Giants with a seemingly impossible third-and-31 from their own 43. Phil Simms dropped back and flipped a little screen pass out to Meggett, who juggled the ball before securing it and took off with blockers in front of him. Meggett juked by a couple of Broncos and then cut back across the field and outran the Denver defenders to the end

> The goal-line stand they made was a big, big key for them. We couldn't knock it in. When you can't make a yard in three tries, then that's very difficult to take. I'll give them credit for keeping us out of there, from scoring in that situation.
>
> —DAN REEVES

zone for a spectacularly unlikely 57-yard score that put New York up 14–0 in the first half.

From there, the Giants' defense took over. In one remarkable sequence in the third quarter, Leonard Marshall, who provided pressure on quarterback John Elway all day, drew two holding calls against Broncos tackle Gerald Perry that wiped out Denver gains of 50 and 22 yards—in addition to the 20 yards in penalties.

Later in the third period, Elway drove the Broncos to the Giants' 1. On third-and-goal from the 1, Bobby Humphrey ran left out of the I-formation and was stopped by linebacker Steve DeOssie just half a yard from the end zone. On fourth down, Humphrey went right from the I-formation, but Gary Reasons read the play perfectly and leapt into the hole where Humphrey was headed, meeting him with a thunderous hit that knocked Humphrey backward while Reasons wrapped him up and sent the Broncos' offense off the field. The two banged helmets so hard that Humphrey's earflap went flying out of his headgear. Parcells said, "It was a big-time hit. It will probably be in the highlight reel." It was the key play of the game.

The Broncos kept up the pressure, with a scrambling Elway passing for 100 of his 292 yards in the final quarter. However, they could only reach pay dirt once—on a 32-yard pass early in the period—and the Giants defense, led by Reasons and Marshall, had ensured a critical victory.

New York then won its last two games to win the Eastern Division crown, but they would lose a heartbreaker to the Rams in the playoffs. Nonetheless, their ferocious, unyielding defense made an unforgettable stand that December day in eight inches of Colorado snow.

Game Details

New York Giants 14 • Denver Broncos 7

Giants	0	14	0	0	14
Broncos	0	0	0	7	7

Date: December 10, 1989

Team Records: Giants 9–4, Broncos 10–3

Scoring Plays:

NYG Anderson 3-yard run (Nittmo PAT)

NYG Meggett 57-yard pass from Simms (Nittmo PAT)

DEN Young 32-yard pass from Elway (Treadwell PAT)

Bill Belichick was one of the architects behind the ferocious Giants defense of the 1980s.
(Photo courtesy of AP Images)

Bill Belichick

That the Giants could come into Denver and shut down the AFC's best team in the snow—after having dropped three of their last four games—was one more example of the brilliance of Bill Belichick as a defensive coach.

In his time in New York, Belichick was called "Doom" by the players for his relentless, abrasive personality, while the writers referred to him as "Captain Sominex" for his deliberately dull and monotonous responses. It was clear that his first love was the Xs and Os of designing different and creative defenses each week, exploiting his opponents' weaknesses through the best usage of his defenders' talents. His own weakness was his personality; he did not yet have Parcells's personal touch with the players.

After a failed five-year tour as head coach in Cleveland, Belichick returned to Parcells's staff in New England and then followed him to the Jets, even briefly becoming the Jets' coach while a deal for compensation for Parcells leaving New England was worked out. When Parcells stepped down as Jets coach to become head of football operations, Belichick was named his successor, but resigned the following day with a brief, bizarre note.

Rather than continue as Parcells's acolyte, Belichick returned to New England, where he has enjoyed control over personnel and found his own voice and remarkable success. Over the years, the Giants have had eight coordinator-level assistant coaches who became head coaches and who led a team to the NFL's championship game. Allie Sherman, Jim Fassel, and John Fox won no titles; Tom Landry and Bill Parcells each won two; Sean Payton has won one; Vince Lombardi won five; and now Belichick's Patriots have won three. Ultimately, he may prove to be the greatest in a long line of great Giants assistant coaches.

October 31, 1999

Trick or Treat

Strahan Completes Halloween Comeback with Overtime Touchdown

Ultimately, 1999 would not be a playoff year for either New York or Philadelphia, but at the midway point of the season, the Giants had hope. They were still in the hunt. With some luck and opportunistic play on this Halloween Sunday, they would head into their bye week with a promising 5–3 record.

By contrast, the Eagles were coming off a 3–13 season and were a slapdash, bumbling bunch under first-year coach Andy Reid in 1999. Yet at halftime, they led the Giants 17–3 on the strength of Duce Staley's 83 rushing yards and an 84-yard touchdown strike from the weak-armed Doug Pederson to Torrance Small, who had slipped by cornerback Jason Sehorn.

The Giants were being beaten soundly and not by giants on the other side of the field. When the players hit the locker room, Jim Fassel tore into their pathetic display with an expletive-laced tirade that caught the attention of the team, and they tightened up their play in the second half.

Midway through the third quarter, the Giants launched a 16-play, 83-yard, nine-minute drive that ended with runner LeShon Johnson going in from the 2-yard

line to put New York within a touchdown of the lead. The plodding Kent Graham–led offense could not add to that, though.

Pederson then got the Eagles in position for a 33-yard field goal with less than eight minutes to play. However, defensive tackle Christian Peter got his hand up and blocked the attempt, preserving the one-score deficit. Again, the Giants could not move the ball. They were forced to punt, but they got another break when Eagles punt returner Allen Rossum let the punt bounce at the 15 and it rolled all the way to the 3.

Penned up on third-and-11 from the 2, Staley took the handoff, was hit immediately by Keith Hamilton and Lyle West, and dropped the ball. New York recovered on the 5, and Graham hit Pete Mitchell for a touchdown to tie the score with two minutes to play. Regulation play ended with the score knotted at 17–17.

In overtime, Christian Peter and Michael Strahan combined for the game-winning play. After a Giants punt, the Eagles were driving, having reached the New York 45. Pederson dropped back to pass, and once again Peter stuck his hand up to deflect the pass. The ball shot straight up in the air. Strahan, who had thus far had a quiet day, found

Michael Strahan celebrates his game-winning overtime interception return in a Halloween matchup against the Eagles in 1999. *(Photo courtesy of AP Images)*

himself in the right place at the right time and made the most of the opportunity. He grabbed the ball and took off 44 yards for the end zone and the winning score, with only heavy-footed linemen in futile pursuit. There, in ground-level end-zone seats of the hostile Veterans Stadium, he found a group of Giants fans, and it was high fives all around.

> **I** was thinking, *It's too good to be true*. It was moving in slow motion. I knew I had to catch it or everyone in New York would hate me right now. But I have good hands. I grabbed it and ran. If you're going to end a game coming back from 14 points down, that's the way to end it.
>
> —MICHAEL STRAHAN

Game Details

New York Giants 23 • Philadelphia Eagles 17

Giants	3	0	0	14	6	**23**
Eagles	3	14	0	0	0	**17**

Date: October 31, 1999

Team Records: Giants 4–3, Eagles 2–5

Scoring Plays:

PHL Johnson 28-yard FG

NYG Blanchard 28-yard FG

PHL Staley 21-yard run (Johnson PAT)

PHL Small 84-yard pass from Pederson (Johnson PAT)

NYG Johnson 2-yard run (Blanchard PAT)

NYG Mitchell 7-yard pass from Graham (Blanchard PAT)

NYG Strahan 44-yard interception return

Michael Strahan

Michael Strahan scored three times during his 15 years in New York and was a bulwark of strength on defense. In the locker room, his signature gap-toothed smile was ever-present, and he was always a receptive interview for the media, win or lose.

The son of a career military man, Strahan was a solid but opinionated citizen after coming to the NFL as a second-round pick out of Texas Southern in 1993. That year, he and fellow rookie Jesse Armstead got to send off Lawrence Taylor and Phil Simms and assume the mantle of team leadership.

However, Strahan was also a moody and overly sensitive player. His teammate Glenn Parker once sarcastically told Mike Freeman of *The New York Times* that he had seen grapes with thicker skin than Strahan. When Tiki Barber publicly criticized Strahan for his contract demands, it created a rift between the two that would never heal.

Even in his moment of greatest triumph, when he set a new single-season sack record with 22.5 in 2001, Strahan engendered criticism because Brett Favre allowed himself to be sacked at the end of the game so that Strahan could break the record. Strahan sacked more than 60 different quarterbacks during his career; he passed Lawrence Taylor as the Giants' all-time leading sacker in 2007. A seven-time Pro Bowl selection, Strahan twice led the NFL in sacks.

While he used a host of different pass-rushing techniques, he was primarily a bull rusher who took advantage of his great strength to push past offensive linemen. Even so, he was equally adept at stopping the run and was the most complete defensive end in the league since Hall of Famer Reggie White. Strahan announced his retirement in June 2008.

Head coach Jim Fassel watches as the Eagles' fourth-quarter field-goal attempt is blocked by lineman Christian Peter. *(Photo courtesy of AP Images)*

November 18, 1985

Taylor Takes Out Theismann

Redskins Lose Quarterback, Giants Lose Game

This 1985 *Monday Night Football* battle for supremacy in the East featured one of the most gruesome plays in NFL history, in which the Redskins lost their veteran starting quarterback Joe Theismann but still won the game. With the help of several trick plays, coach Joe Gibbs led Washington to victory over New York behind an untried backup quarterback who had already failed at professional baseball before hooking on with the Redskins.

The Redskins scored first after a fake punt by Steve Cox kept their drive alive, and Theismann hit tight end Don Warren for the touchdown. The Giants evened the score in the first quarter on a two-play, 80-yard drive that consisted of a 24-yard interference call on the

Redskins' Vernon Dean and a 56-yard run by Joe Morris on a trap play.

On the second play of the second period, Gibbs dialed up another trick play, but he would forever regret this one. Theismann handed off to John Riggins near midfield, and Riggins flipped the ball back to Theismann for a flea flicker, but the Giants were not fooled. Harry Carson was in on Theismann immediately, but Joe eluded him. From behind, Lawrence Taylor jumped on Theismann's back. As the quarterback went down, his right leg got caught in an awkward position and bent the wrong way. From the other side, Gary Reasons hit Theismann low while Jim Burt came in over the top. Theismann's lower tibia and fibula snapped like kindling.

Taylor and Burt immediately realized what had happened and began signaling furiously to the Washington bench for medical assistance.

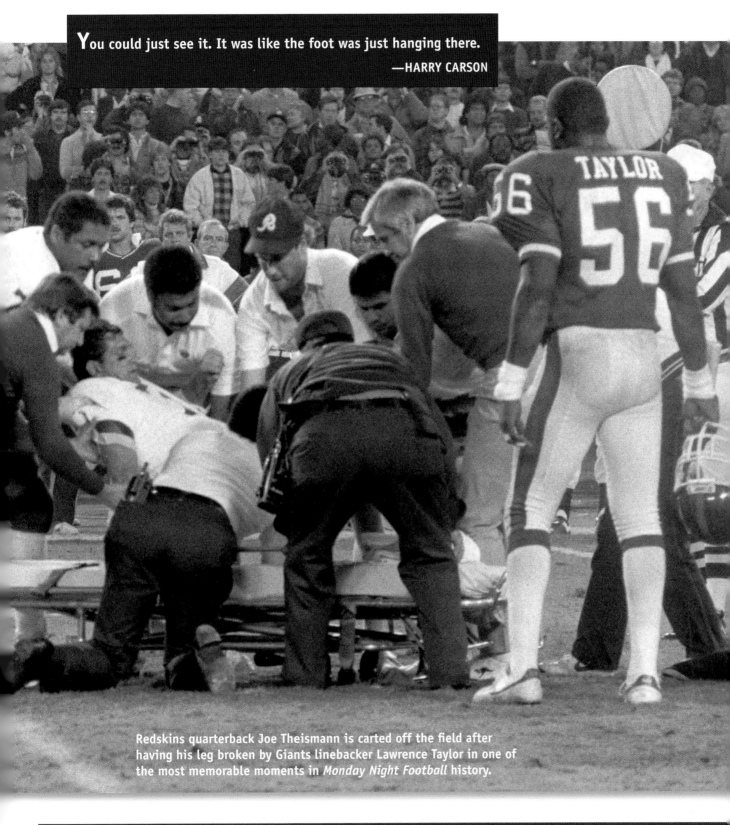

Redskins quarterback Joe Theismann is carted off the field after having his leg broken by Giants linebacker Lawrence Taylor in one of the most memorable moments in *Monday Night Football* history.

Taylor held his head in his hands and thought to himself, *What have I done?*

Theismann was wheeled off the field. His career was over, but the game continued on, with rookie Jay Schroeder taking over at quarterback. Schroeder's first pass went for a 44-yard gain, but a Redskins fumble ended that drive, leaving the game 7–7 at the half.

Washington opened the second half with an onside kick by Steve Cox, who recovered it himself. John Riggins scored four plays later to take the lead. The Giants rebounded, with Joe Morris scoring two more touchdowns in the third quarter on a 41-yard trap play and an eight-yard run following a fumble recovery to retake the lead 21–14.

Washington staged a comeback in the final period on a Mark Moseley field goal followed by a second Steve Cox onside kick with more than 11 minutes to play. Again, the Redskins recovered the kick and this time drove down to score on a Schroeder pass to tight end Clint Didier. The Giants were unable to mount any more offense, and the Redskins held on for the Pyrrhic victory.

Game Details

New York Giants 21 • Washington Redskins 23

Giants	7	0	14	0	**21**
Redskins	7	0	7	9	**23**

Date: November 18, 1985

Team Records: Giants 7–3, Redskins 5–5

Scoring Plays:

WSH Warren 10-yard pass from Theismann (Moseley PAT)

NYG Morris 56-yard run (Schubert PAT)

WSH Riggins 1-yard run (Moseley PAT)

NYG Morris 41-yard run (Schubert PAT)

NYG Morris 8-yard run (Schubert PAT)

WSH Moseley 28-yard FG

WSH Didier 14-yard pass from Schroeder (Moseley kick failed)

Harry Carson

The Giants drafted Harry Carson out of South Carolina State as a defensive end in the fourth round in 1976. Converted to middle linebacker by position coach Marty Schottenheimer and then to an inside linebacker in the 3-4 defense in 1979, Harry played between Brad Van Pelt and Brian Kelley until 1984, when both were traded. Harry walked out of training camp soon after.

Bill Parcells tweaked him by telling the press that he hoped Carson was going to the library to look up the word *leadership*, and Harry returned two days later. In truth, Parcells relied heavily on Carson and defensive end George Martin as veteran leaders, and those two teammates would retire together in 1988.

A nine-time Pro Bowl player, Harry was a premier run stuffer who once made 20 tackles in a game against the Packers in 1982. As he stated simply in his autobiography, *Point of Attack*, "My job is knocking people down. I'm a linebacker in the National Football League. And I'm good at my job...I rarely do anything spectacular. I hardly ever blitz the quarterback. I stop the run. I wrap running backs up and lay them down."

After six unsuccessful campaigns as a Hall of Fame finalist, the proud old linebacker wrote to the selection committee in 2005, saying he no longer wanted to be considered for election. The following year, Harry was elected and dropped his public reluctance because he knew how much Wellington Mara had wanted to see him enshrined. Harry Carson indeed understood leadership; he was the heart and soul of the New York Giants for more than a dozen years.

Linebacker Harry Carson was a leader on defense and was eventually elected to the Pro Football Hall of Fame.

Much-maligned cornerback Corey Webster picks off Brett Favre on the second play of overtime, setting up Lawrence Tyne's game-winning field goal that sent the Giants to Super Bowl XLII.

January 20, 2008

Super Cool

Webster's Overtime Interception Brings Redemption and Victory Over the Packers

The story of the 2007 NFL season was the explosive New England Patriots' attempt at an undefeated season. In the final week of the season, the 15–0 Patriots came to the Meadowlands, with both the Pats and Giants having already clinched their playoff seeding. Other teams in similar situations around the league were resting starters. However, the Patriots had committed to playing 60 minutes each game all year, so there was no doubt they would be going all out. To his credit, Tom Coughlin played his starters and went for the win as well. Despite losing 38–35 to New England in one of the best games of the year, the Giants gained league-wide respect and launched themselves on a stunning road playoff run.

New York had a losing record at home, but its steadily improving defense helped pave a 7–1 road record. In the wild-card round, the Giants took apart a well-rested but weak Tampa Bay team 24–14. In the divisional round, the Giants outlasted a well-rested but disorganized top-seeded Cowboys team 21–17. For the conference championship, the Giants would have to travel to frigid Green Bay where the second-seeded Packers, who had taken a middle route by resting some starters in the finale, waited.

At kickoff, the temperature at Lambeau Field was minus-2 degrees with a minus-23 wind chill; it was the third-coldest game in recorded NFL history. The first time New York had the ball, the team drove 71 yards in 14 plays and bled nearly eight minutes off the clock in taking a 3–0 lead. This drive set the tone for the Giants, with its sure-handed mix of runs and passes, especially passes from Eli Manning to the uncoverable Plaxico Burress, who would catch 11 balls on the day to set a team playoff record.

A short drive to open the second quarter led to a second Lawrence Tynes field goal. However, the 6–0 lead was short-lived as Green Bay scored on the most spectacular play of the day immediately following the kickoff. From the Green Bay 10, Brett Favre dropped back to pass. Receiver Donald Driver pushed past an attempted chuck by cornerback Corey Webster and broke free as Webster slid to the ground. Favre hit a wide-open Driver around the 30, and he outraced Webster for the goal line on a 90-yard touchdown. The momentum seemed to be turning as Green Bay forced New York to punt on its next two possessions, and then drove to the Giants' 19 where Favre threw a screen pass to Brandon Jackson with two blockers in front of him. In a key stop, middle linebacker Antonio Pierce outflanked guard Jason Spitz and made the tackle for a one-yard gain. Green Bay settled for a field goal and a 10–6 halftime lead.

New York received the second-half kickoff and took more than seven minutes to drive 69 yards for the go-ahead touchdown on a short run by Brandon Jacobs. Favre answered with a second touchdown pass to retake the lead, but Manning marched the Giants right back down the field for a 20–17 lead. Green Bay knotted the game at 20 early in the fourth quarter on a drive that was aided by Packers tackle Mark Tauscher's fumble recovery after Giants cornerback R.W. McQuarters picked off Favre, but lost the handle on the ball. Manning, who looked quite comfortable throwing the ball in the frosty conditions, again took the Giants deep into Packers territory, but Tynes missed a 43-yard field goal with less than seven minutes to play. Favre, who looked older and older as the game went on, was unable to move the Packers, and Manning gave Tynes a second chance from 36 yards with four seconds to play.

Game Details

New York Giants 23 • Green Bay Packers 20

Giants	3	3	14	0	3	**23**
Packers	0	10	7	3	0	**20**

Date: January 20, 2008
Team Records: Giants 10–6, Packers 13–3
Scoring Plays:
NYG Tynes 29-yard FG
NYG Tynes 37-yard FG
GBP Driver 90-yard pass from Favre (Crosby PAT)
GBP Crosby 36-yard FG
NYG Jacobs 1-yard run (Tynes PAT)
GBP Lee 12-yard pass from Favre (Crosby PAT)
NYG Bradshaw 4-yard run (Tynes PAT)
GBP Crosby 37-yard FG
NYG Tynes 47-yard FG

Tom Coughlin

The extreme chill of the weather was clear on this evening in Green Bay from the deepening red on Tom Coughlin's cheeks, but he probably didn't even notice the cold as he watched his Giants playing the game the way he had wanted them to all along. Just one year before, it was widely suspected that Coughlin would be fired for the underachieving performance of his noisy, out-of-control players.

The Giants hired him to run a tighter ship than his predecessor Jim Fassel did. Coughlin instituted an intense, autocratic atmosphere where "on time" meant 5-10 minutes early, but it took the retirement of Tiki Barber and an injury to Jeremy Shockey to be fully accepted by the players. In 2007, Coughlin softened his approach a bit and hired dynamic new defensive coordinator Steve Spagnuolo to turn things around. In the playoffs, the Giants at last played as a team, with few turnovers and penalties, all units contributing equally and without finger-pointing and selfish emotional displays. With the team's recent history, no one expected that to last for a four-game playoff run, but Coughlin took this underrated team all the way to the Super Bowl.

In 2008, Coughlin's Giants went 12–4 but lost to the Eagles in the first round of the playoffs. The following season, they were 5–0 before collapsing and missing the postseason.

We like it on the road. Our guys have heart. They're something. They never say die and find a way to win.

—TOM COUGHLIN

The 2007 season was sweet redemption for embattled head coach Tom Coughlin.

After a bad snap by Jay Alford, though, Tynes missed a second time. Overtime.

Green Bay won the coin toss and started at their own 26. On the second play from scrimmage, the Packers ran a play they had run three times earlier in the game. Tight end Donald Lee shifted back into the backfield before the snap while Donald Driver moved up to the line. While it appeared that Lee would act as a lead-blocking full-back on a run, instead Favre dropped back and threw an out pattern. The play had worked twice before—but not this time. Cornerback Corey Webster stayed right with Driver and was in perfect position to jump the pattern and intercept Favre's underthrown pass at the 43. A skittering nine-yard return gave the Giants the ball at the Green Bay 34. Two runs by Ahmad Bradshaw placed the ball at the 29, and Tynes nailed the 47-yard field goal. Tynes and Corey Webster had their atonement, and New York had a rematch with the undefeated 18–0 Patriots.

December 7, 1958

Svare Swats Lions Away

Blocked Field Goal Seals Giants Win

The surging second-place Giants came to Detroit in Week 11 of the 1958 season to face the struggling defending champion Lions. New York needed a victory to keep alive its hopes of overtaking the Browns for the Eastern crown. On a gray, 15-degree Michigan day that featured several unlikely plays, the Giants toughed out a win.

New York scored twice in the opening period. First, defensive end Jim Katcavage dumped Lions runner Gene Gedman in the end zone for a safety, and then Pat Summerall added a field goal for a 5–0 lead. Safety Jimmy Patton set up the Giants' third score by recovering a Lions fumble at the 19-yard line in the second quarter. Charley Conerly hit Alex Webster for a six-yard touchdown to extend the lead to 12–0, but Detroit's Jim Martin booted a field goal before the half to narrow the lead.

In the third quarter, Detroit gained control of the game. Quarterback Tobin Rote—cousin to the Giants' Kyle Rote—led the Lions to the Giants' 2 and then

hit Ken Webb with a touchdown pass. Soon after, Conerly fumbled in trying a handoff to Mel Triplett at his own 34; linebacker Wayne Walker scooped up the ball and ran it in for another touchdown and the 17–12 lead.

Lions head coach George Wilson derailed his team's momentum early in the fourth quarter. Facing a fourth-and-21 from his own 44, Wilson ordered a fake for punter Yale Lary. Lary took off running but was collared by Cliff Livingston on a diving tackle after gaining just a yard, drawing hearty booing from the stands. This play call appeared so fishy that afterward NFL commissioner Bert Bell was called on to defend it and deny it was influenced by gambling interests.

On the next play, Conerly hit Bob Schnelker for a 34-yard gain to the Lions' 11. On fourth-and-one from the 2, the Giants went for it. Conerly handed off to Frank Gifford, and he punched in the lead-changing score over right tackle.

Down 19–17, Tobin Rote drove the Lions down the field in a two-minute drill that stalled at the

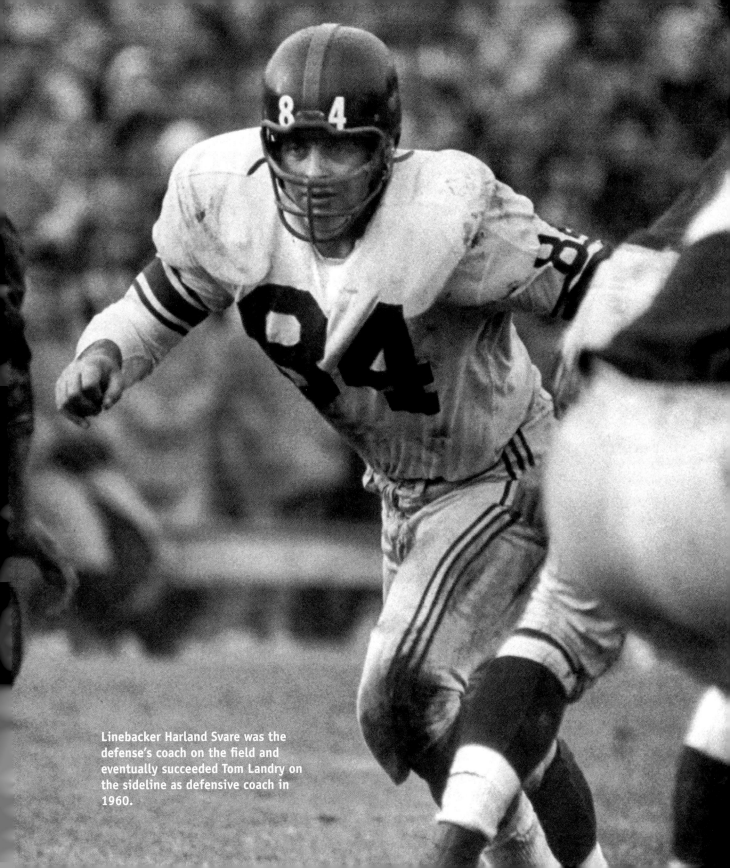

Linebacker Harland Svare was the defense's coach on the field and eventually succeeded Tom Landry on the sideline as defensive coach in 1960.

Giants' 18. On fourth down, Jim Martin and the field-goal unit came onto the field with 1:21 to play. With the season in the balance, Giants veterans Andy Robustelli and Harland Svare discussed the situation and decided the best approach was for Robustelli to drive Lions lineman Gerald Perry inside, giving Svare an angle to shoot in and get his arms up. When the ball was snapped, Robustelli took Perry out and Svare shot through the gap. Svare didn't even have to dive as he blocked Martin's kick with his left wrist, and the game and season were saved. On this great play, the steadfast Giants defense had risen to the occasion once again.

> **N**othing doing. I'll block the kick. You have a better blocking angle than I will. You drive him inside.
>
> —HARLAND SVARE TO ANDY ROBUSTELLI,
> QUOTED IN *THE NEW YORK TIMES*

Game Details

New York Giants 19 • Detroit Lions 17

Giants	5	7	0	7	**19**
Lions	0	3	14	0	**17**

Date: December 7, 1958

Team Records: Giants 7–3, Lions 4–5–1

Scoring Plays:

NYG Katcavage tackled Gedman for safety

NYG Summerall 18-yard FG

NYG Webster 6-yard pass from Conerly (Summerall PAT)

DET Martin 39-yard FG

DET Webb 2-yard pass from Rote (Martin PAT)

DET Walker 34-yard fumble recovery (Martin PAT)

NYG Gifford 1-yard run (Summerall PAT)

Dee-Fense

Defensive coach Tom Landry had warned defensive end Jim Katcavage that he needed to line up wide to defend against Tobin Rote's rollouts. That tip put him in position to drop Gene Gedman for a first-quarter safety that provided the winning margin in the game. This was just the sort of play that Giants fans came to expect in the late 1950s, when their "Dee-Fense" chants echoed throughout Yankee Stadium and inspired the first truly celebrated defense in the sport's history during the Giants' championship run from 1956 through 1963.

It was also the first 4-3 defense in pro football, a base defense devised by Landry that is still the base scheme for most NFL teams 50 years later. Landry's defense took full advantage of the immense talent on hand. The four-man defensive line was the very first "fearsome foursome." Ends Katcavage and Andy Robustelli were rangy and quick. Tackle Roosevelt Grier was a gentle giant who tended to play just as well as he needed to, while the stumpy Dick Modzelewski was more fiery.

The 4-3 was crafted to funnel plays to the middle linebacker position, where Sam Huff was a hard tackler and natural leader with a reputation for playing mean.

The secondary was anchored by ball-hawking safeties Emlen Tunnell and Jimmy Patton. The cornerbacks of 1958, Ed Hughes and Carl Karilivacz, were supplanted by Lindon Crow and Dick Lynch in 1959, and Crow was replaced by Erich Barnes in 1961.

The years of 1956 to 1963 were a great period in Giants history, and their aptly feted defense was a major reason why.

Tom Landry's 4-3 defense and a key field-goal block by Harland Svare (left, kneeling) led the Giants to a win over the Lions in 1958. *(Photo courtesy of AP Images)*

November 25, 1982

Taylor Turns Lions into Turkeys

97-Yard Interception Return Wins Thanksgiving Game

The 1982 NFL season featured an ugly players' strike, during which Weeks 3 through 9 were canceled. The NFL returned on Sunday, November 21, and the Giants promptly lost to the Redskins, falling to 0–3 just one season after making the playoffs for the first time in 18 years. Even worse, Lawrence Taylor, the team's second-year superstar linebacker, was listed as doubtful with a sprained knee for the next game—just four days later on Thanksgiving Day, against the Lions.

Indeed, Taylor did not start, and the Lions scored twice on field goals set up by interceptions to take a 6–0 lead in the second quarter. Drawn by the needs of his team and the national stage of the annual Turkey Day contest, Taylor replaced Byron Hunt in the second quarter. In the third quarter, he started to impose his will on the Lions, and the game became the Lawrence Taylor Show.

Early in the second half, Taylor blitzed and forced Lions quarterback Gary Danielson to get off an ill-advised, hurried pass that Harry Carson picked off and returned to the Detroit 41-yard line. Six plays later, kicker Joe Danelo made the score 6–3. On the first play after the ensuing kickoff, Taylor exploded on Lions ball carrier Billy Sims and knocked the ball loose. Brad Van Pelt recovered it at the Detroit 18. Although the inept Giants offense, led by Scott Brunner, still could not move the ball, Danelo came on to kick another field goal to tie the game.

The next time the Lions had the ball, Taylor blitzed again, grabbed Danielson by the jersey with one hand, and tossed him to the ground, forcing a punt.

Despite an ailing knee, Lawrence Taylor converted a 97-yard interception return for a touchdown against the Lions. *(Photo courtesy of WireImages)*

In the fourth quarter, the Lions finally got a drive going and moved to the New York 4. At this critical moment in a tie game, Lawrence Taylor made the biggest play of the day. On third down, running back Horace King and tight end David Hill ran crisscrossing routes to confuse Taylor and fellow linebacker Brian Kelley. Kelley followed Taylor's original man, Hill, as he was supposed to do. To bait Danielson, Taylor faked that he was staying with Hill, but he then closed on his new man, King, with the pass in the air. L.T. caught the ball at the 3 and went into a sprint down the sideline, sore knee notwithstanding. At the 50, Taylor noticed defensive coordinator Bill Parcells on the sideline motioning to keep running, and he did, with Danielson and Dexter Bussey in distant pursuit. Although there was a penalty on the play, it was against King for offensive pass interference, so the touchdown stood.

The 97-yard interception return was the third longest in team history. It proved to be the winning score and only touchdown in the Giants' 13–6 defensive victory. New York would end the season 4–5 and out of the playoffs, but 1982 remains memorable for the Thanksgiving game that Lawrence Taylor won all by himself.

Game Details

New York Giants 13 • Detroit Lions 6

Giants	0	0	6	7	**13**
Lions	3	3	0	0	**6**

Date: November 25, 1982

Team Records: Giants 0–3, Lions 2–1

Scoring Plays:

DET Murray 46-yard FG

DET Murray 44-yard FG

NYG Danelo 34-yard FG

NYG Danelo 40-yard FG

NYG Taylor 97-yard interception return (Danelo PAT)

The ball in my hand took care of all the pain from the injury.
—LAWRENCE TAYLOR

Coach Bill Parcells's motivational skills helped Lawrence Taylor become arguably the greatest linebacker in NFL history. (*Photo courtesy of WireImages*)

Lawrence Taylor

Lawrence Taylor terrorized quarterbacks primarily as a pass rusher. This interception against the Lions was one of only nine he would record in his 13 years in the NFL. He was the definition of an impact player, and he forced opponents to gameplan against him. Coach Joe Gibbs of the division-rival Redskins devised the H-back—a combination tight end and offensive lineman—as a direct counter to the havoc Taylor wrought. Washington's formations were always crafted to try to get two blockers on Taylor, and other teams followed suit.

Taylor was the second player taken in the 1981 draft; he proved his value by recording 133 tackles and 9.5 sacks in that first season. For that, he was named both Rookie of the Year and Defensive Player of the Year. Taylor would go on to be named Defensive Player of the Year three more times; he also won the NFL MVP Award in 1986. For seven consecutive seasons, he recorded double-digit sack totals, leading the league with 20.5 sacks in 1986.

During his career, Taylor was named to 10 Pro Bowls, recorded 142 sacks, forced 33 fumbles, and recovered 11 more. He was a ferocious tackler and unrelenting in pursuit of the play. L.T. combined the speed of a back and the strength of a lineman, along with quickness, agility, and intensity.

Off the field, Taylor had outsized appetites that put him in and out of rehab several times, both during and after his playing career. This sordid side caused some controversy when he became eligible for the Hall of Fame, but no one could deny his greatness on the football field. He was enshrined in Canton in 1999.

Some consider him the greatest defensive player in NFL history; most would concede he was the finest linebacker. Without question, he is the greatest player the Giants have ever had, and his No. 56 jersey has been retired.

November 23, 1986

Martin Entraps Elway

Lineman Scores Giants' Only Touchdown in Win over Denver

Just one week after the last-minute heroics against the Vikings, the 1986 Giants were at it again against a tough Broncos squad on a late November day at the Meadowlands. New York was trying to win its fifth straight game for the second time that year, and they relied on the big play for this battle.

In this nail-biter, the Broncos kicked a field goal on their first possession. The Giants answered with their own three-pointer by Raul Allegre on the first play of the second quarter, capping a 16-play, 63-yard drive. Denver got a break late in the period when Stacy Robinson fumbled at the Broncos' 18-yard line. Denver turned that into another field goal, aided by a 39-yard interference call on Perry Williams. Quarterback John Elway had the Broncos on the move again in the closing seconds of the half—until defensive end George Martin altered the course of the game.

George Martin picks off John Elway and lumbers toward the goal line late in the first half on November 23, 1986. It was the seventh career touchdown for Martin, and the only Giants touchdown of the game. *(Photo courtesy of AP Images)*

Game Details

New York Giants 19 • Denver Broncos 16

Broncos	3	3	3	7	**16**
Giants	0	10	3	6	**19**

Date: November 23, 1986

Team Records: Giants 9–2, Broncos 9–2

Scoring Plays:

DEN Karlis 40-yard FG

NYG Allegre 31-yard FG

DEN Karlis 32-yard FG

NYG Martin 78-yard interception return (Allegre PAT)

NYG Allegre 45-yard FG

DEN Karlis 42-yard FG

NYG Allegre 46-yard FG

DEN Winder 4-yard run (Karlis PAT)

NYG Allegre 34-yard FG

On first down from the New York 13, Elway tried to loft a swing pass to Gerald Willhite, but he didn't factor in the agility of Martin, who had played basketball at the University of Oregon. Martin had gotten by tackle Ken Lanier and jumped to bat the pass back to himself. Grabbing the interception, he turned upfield at the 22. Elway had the angle on Martin at the 35, and George held the ball in his outstretched right hand, hoping to lateral it to Lawrence Taylor. Elway grabbed for Martin high to prevent the lateral, but Martin switched hands and shoved the quarterback down with his right arm at the 50. With Taylor and Harry Carson leading interference, Martin plodded on. At the 20, Mark Collins raced in to knock down the last Broncos player, Sammy Winder. Martin leapfrogged Winder at the 15 and trudged into the end zone as an elated L.T. leaped on his back and tackled him. The 78-yard play took a full 17 seconds, and it gave the Giants the lead.

In the third quarter, the teams exchanged field goals, and Allegre booted still another field goal five minutes into the final period, making the score 16–9. However, Elway brought the Broncos back with one of his patented fourth-quarter drives. Denver traveled 73 yards in nine plays and scored the tying touchdown on a Winder run with 1:55 to go.

Phil Simms had had a quiet day, so it was time for him to go to work. Quickly, though, he faced a third-and-21 from his own 18. With the dangerous Elway on the other sideline, the Giants needed a first down. They called a double-seam route, in which both wide receivers run straight up the seam of the zone coverage. Just like the previous week on fourth-and-17 against the Vikings, Simms found Bobby Johnson at the crucial time, and Johnson caught the ball for a 24-yard gain to the 42. Two plays later, from their 39, Simms tried the double-seam again and found Phil McConkey for a 46-yard gain to the Broncos' 15. With only six seconds left, Allegre came in and kicked the 34-yard game-winning field goal.

The Giants were in the midst of a 12-game winning streak and were starting to believe they were a team of destiny. They would meet the Broncos again in the Super Bowl and complete their mission by winning the franchise's first NFL title in 30 years.

> **W**hen I caught it, it was a bright sunny day. When I got to the end zone, it was cloudy. The weather had changed considerably.
>
> —GEORGE MARTIN

George Martin

George Martin intercepted three passes in his career, and he returned each one for a touchdown. Martin also scored on two fumble recoveries, a lateral after a blocked field goal, and a pass reception as a tight end during his 14 years as a Giants defensive end. He also tackled John Elway for a safety in the Super Bowl. Only Jason Taylor scored more times as a defensive lineman.

The undersized Martin was a lowly 11th-round draft pick in 1975, but he became a starter at defensive end in his second season. When the Giants switched to the 3-4 defense in 1981 under new defensive coordinator Bill Parcells, the quick and nimble Martin became a situational pass-rushing specialist. He is credited with 46 career sacks from the time sacks began to be officially counted in 1982, but is thought to have accumulated more than 80 sacks unofficially.

In the Super Bowl season of 1986, Martin returned to the starting lineup at age 33 and had an excellent year, capped by that Super Bowl safety. Having lived through some very bad years with the Giants, he and longtime teammate Harry Carson were respected team leaders who appreciated that first championship even more than most of their teammates.

Martin was an unselfish teammate who co-founded the team's Bible study group; he was the Giants' candidate for the league's community service Whizzer White Award for 10 consecutive years. (He finally won the award in 1987.) He and Carson both retired after the 1988 season, but Martin has stayed active with the Giants and in the local community. In 2007, he embarked on a 3,000-mile walk across the U.S. to raise money for 9/11 rescue and recovery workers.

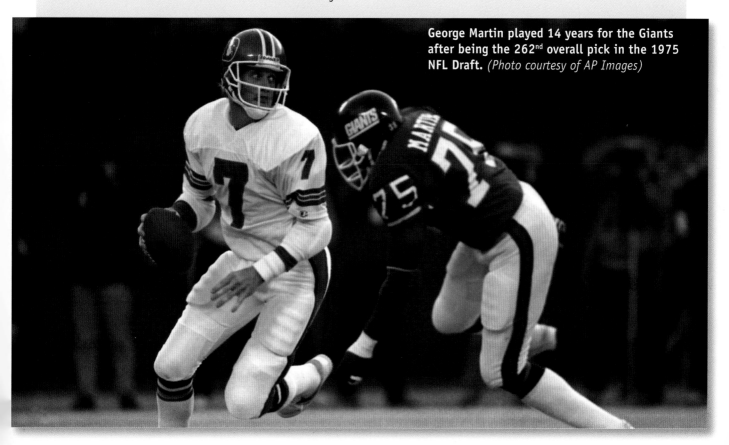

George Martin played 14 years for the Giants after being the 262nd overall pick in the 1975 NFL Draft. *(Photo courtesy of AP Images)*

December 19, 1981

In the Hunt for the Playoffs after 18 Years

Key Pick Leads to Overtime Win

The Giants went into their 1981 season finale against the 12–3 Dallas Cowboys with an 8–7 record. It was the third season for general manager George Young and head coach Ray Perkins, and it was time for the team to produce. A win over the vaunted Cowboys would not only mean just the third winning season in the past 18 for the Giants, but it would also keep their hopes alive for ending an 18-year playoff drought. Although it may not have been clear at the time, 1981 was a turning-point season for New York—it was Lawrence Taylor's rookie year, and it marked the return of Bill Parcells to the Giants as defensive coordinator. That pairing would bring a renaissance to the franchise in the coming decade.

The fired-up Giants came out smoking on this clear, 25-degree Saturday with the wind gusting to 23 miles an hour, and they held Dallas to just 41 yards of total offense in the first half. However, two potential Giants scoring drives ended in missed field goals into the wind by the usually reliable Joe Danelo: a 21-yarder was wide left and a 27-yarder was wide right. Danelo also plunked one off the upright, but that was erased by a penalty.

Finally, with five minutes to go in the third quarter, a 20-yard touchdown pass from Scott Brunner to Tom Mullady capped a six-play, 62-yard drive and gave New York the first lead. Dallas then took the ensuing kickoff and drove 80 yards in 11 plays to tie the game on a three-yard lob to Doug Cosbie. On the Giants' next possession, Brunner was intercepted by Michael Downs, and Dallas kicked a field goal to take a 10-7 lead with nine minutes to play.

As has often been the case in Giants history, it was the defense to the rescue, forcing turnovers on the Cowboys' last three possessions of the game. With 2:08 left, rookie linebacker Byron Hunt knocked loose a pitchout to Tony Dorsett and defensive end George Martin recovered it on the Dallas 45-yard line. After converting a fourth-and-13

Joe Danelo's overtime field goal gave the Giants a 13–10 victory over the Dallas Cowboys at Giants Stadium in 1981. *(Photo courtesy of AP Images)*

on a 21-yard pass to John Mistler, New York was in position for a field goal, and Danelo tied the game with a 40-yarder with 30 seconds to play in regulation.

On Dallas's first possession in the overtime period, Dorsett bobbled another pitchout. Lawrence Taylor engulfed him and came away with the football at the Dallas 40. Brunner ran a bootleg on an audible and got all the way to the 17, but Danelo bounced another kick off the upright on his 33-yard try into the wind. Two plays later came the play of the game. On second down, Lawrence Taylor blitzed Danny White and forced him to scramble. White unwisely unloaded a weak pass toward Butch Johnson, but Hunt glided over, snagged the interception at the 31, and returned it to the 24. Three plays later, at 6:19 of the overtime period, Danelo knocked one straight and true from 35 yards out to give the Giants the 13–10 victory. Coach Perkins was so excited that he helped carry his kicker off the field.

The Giants had their winning season. The next day at Shea Stadium, the Jets beat the Packers, sending the Giants to the postseason for the first time since 1963.

Byron Hunt picked off a Danny White pass to set up Joe Danelo's game-winning field goal in 1981.

Game Details

New York Giants 13 • Dallas Cowboys 10

Cowboys	0	0	0	10	0	**10**
Giants	0	0	7	3	3	**13**

Date: December 19, 1981

Team Records: Giants 8–7, Cowboys 12–3

Scoring Plays:

NYG Mullady 20-yard pass from Brunner (Danelo PAT)

DAL Cosbie 3-yard pass from White (Septien PAT)

DAL Septien 36-yard FG

NYG Danelo 40-yard FG

NYG Danelo 35-yard FG

The Linebackers

New York has been blessed with some of the very best sets of linebackers ever to play professional football, right from the start of the 4-3 defense that Tom Landry implemented in New York in 1956.

When Ray Perkins became coach in 1979, he saw the strength at the linebacker position and instituted the 3-4 defense. The transition was complete in 1981, with Bill Parcells coaching the linebackers and future Hall of Famer Lawrence Taylor joining the team. Parcells, as head coach in 1984, wanted more youth and speed, so he replaced aging veterans Brad Van Pelt and Brian Kelley with Byron Hunt and Gary Reasons.

The inconsistent Byron Hunt was beaten out by All-Pro Carl Banks two years later. Three years after that, All-Pro Pepper Johnson replaced the retiring Harry Carson, with Gary Reasons taking over as signal caller. The linebacking during this golden era was so good that backups such as Hunt, Andy Headen, Johnie Cooks, and Steve DeOssie would have started on many teams throughout the NFL.

Consistent across all eras, though, was the aggressive intensity of Giants linebackers, best expressed by Lawrence Taylor on the sideline during one game: "Let's go out there like a bunch of crazed dogs."

Lawrence Taylor and Pepper Johnson were at the center of some of the best linebacking corps in NFL history. (*Photo courtesy of AP Images*)

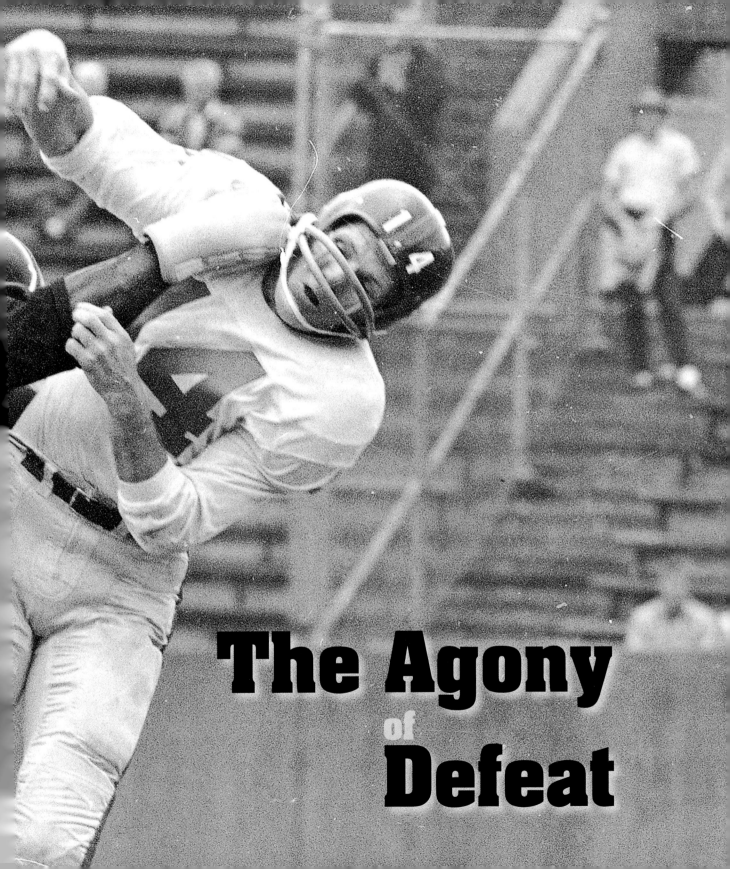

The Agony
of
Defeat

December 28, 1958

Giants' 87-Yard Pass Play Falls Short

Colts Capture Title in Sudden Death

It has come to be known as "The Greatest Game Ever Played," but it was never that, especially not for Giants fans. The 1958 NFL Championship Game was the first title game to end regulation play in a tie and force a sudden-death overtime period, and thus it had an exciting conclusion. However, the game between the Giants and the Baltimore Colts was filled with fumbles and miscues on both sides and was hardly the best game played by either team that season. What captivated a national television audience was the expert execution of the two-minute offense by a young Johnny Unitas to tie the game, and then his relentless march in overtime for the win.

Colts back Alan Ameche scores the winning touchdown in overtime of the 1958 NFL Championship Game, also known as "The Greatest Game Ever Played." *(Photo courtesy of AP Images)*

Alex Webster

It wasn't surprising that Alex Webster was in the right place at the right time on the spectacular 87-yard pass play that got the Giants going in the third quarter. The tough New Jersey native was someone his teammates could always depend upon to make the big play at crunch time.

Webster was an 11th-round draft pick of the Redskins in 1953; they tried him on defense before cutting him. Webster headed to Montreal, where he became a star and led the CFL in rushing in 1954. The Giants noticed him when they were scouting Montreal quarterback Sam Etcheverry. They signed Alex in 1955.

The determined Webster led the team in rushing as a rookie halfback. He had an effective, gliding running style and used his blocks very well, and he would fight for every yard when the blocking disappeared. He also had a determined nose for the goal line; until recent years, his 56 touchdowns rushing and receiving were only exceeded by Giants Frank Gifford and Joe Morrison.

Shoulder and leg injuries from 1958 through 1960 nearly got Webster cut in training camp in 1961. However, after being switched to fullback by Allie Sherman, Webster had his two biggest seasons before he began to show the signs of age in 1963, at age 32. He led the Giants in rushing three times and retired as their all-time leading rusher. A popular figure with the fans, Webster went on to coach the team in the post-Sherman era with limited success, finishing with a 29–40–1 record.

Despite having beaten the Colts seven weeks before, the Giants were 3.5-point underdogs on this mild December day at Yankee Stadium. New York boasted the NFL's best defense, but Baltimore had the second-best defense to go with the highest-scoring offense in the league. The Giants were just ninth in points scored and were worn down from having to win a playoff game over the Browns the week before to get to the championship game.

The two starting quarterbacks, Unitas and Don Heinrich, traded fumbles in the first quarter and then Unitas was intercepted by Carl Karilivacz, but New York was forced to punt. The Colts' offense could be explosive, and Unitas proved that by quickly hitting Lenny Moore for a 60-yard bomb. However, the Giants defense stiffened, and Colts kicker Steve Myhra missed a 26-yard field goal.

The Giants followed the unusual practice of keeping Charley Conerly on the sideline at the outset of games to observe, as backup quarterback Heinrich probed the opposing defense. Conerly now entered the game and led

Game Details

New York Giants 17 • Baltimore Colts 23

Colts	0	14	0	3	6	**23**
Giants	3	0	7	7	0	**17**

Date: December 28, 1958

Team Records: Giants 10–3, Colts 9–3

Scoring Plays:

NYG Summerall 36-yard FG

BAL Ameche 2-yard run (Myhra PAT)

BAL Berry 15-yard pass from Unitas (Myhra PAT)

NYG Triplett 1-yard run (Summerall PAT)

NYG Gifford 15-yard pass from Conerly (Summerall PAT)

BAL Myhra 20-yard FG

BAL Ameche 1-yard run

Kyle Rote

The man who traveled the farthest with the ball on that 87-yard play from the 1958 championship game was receiver Kyle Rote, who caught the pass and went 52 yards before losing the ball on a rare fumble. Rote was a big-play receiver for New York. His mark of 48 receiving touchdowns held up as the team record for 47 years, until Amani Toomer exceeded it in 2007.

Rote got his first national recognition as a junior at Southern Methodist, when he substituted for All-American Doak Walker and nearly beat the heavily favored Notre Dame single-handedly. In his senior year, Kyle was runner-up for the Heisman Trophy. The Giants nabbed him as the bonus pick at the top of the 1951 draft.

As a rookie, the running back tore up his knee in training camp and played little. He showed promise in his second season, but then he tore up his other knee in 1953, and his career as a running back was over practically before it began. Tom Landry noted how well Rote ran pass patterns, though, and suggested Kyle switch to end. That move rescued his career.

> **I** didn't really fumble. The guy pulled the ball away. But there it was on the goddamn ground, and I just went numb. You know what? Thank God for Alex Webster.
>
> —KYLE ROTE,
>
> IN *THE GAME OF THEIR LIVES* BY DAVE KLEIN

Rote would play in four Pro Bowls. He had his greatest years at the end of his career, when Allie Sherman began to open up the offense. Rote caught the most passes of his 11-year tenure as a Giant in his final season, with 53 in 1961. He finished as the all-time leader in receptions and receiving yards for the Giants. He was an intelligent, talented man who was so universally admired by his teammates that many of them named sons after him. After retiring as a football player, he had a long, successful career in broadcasting.

the Giants into Colts territory for Pat Summerall to kick a 36-yard field goal with two minutes left in the first period.

Early in the second quarter, Frank Gifford lost a fumble at his own 20-yard line, and the Colts capitalized to take a 7–3 lead. The Giants were forced to punt from midfield on their next possession, but Baltimore's Jackie Simpson fumbled on the return and the Giants had the ball on the Colts' 10. Once again, Frank Gifford lost the handle. Baltimore got the ball back and drove 86 yards in 15 plays to score on a 15-yard pass to Raymond Berry. The Giants went to the locker room at the half trailing 14–3 and having been outgained 198 yards to 86.

After an exchange of punts to begin the third quarter, the Colts mounted another drive. With a first-and-goal at the New York 3, it looked as if the game were about to turn into a rout. After three dive plays moved the ball just two yards, however, Unitas tried something different on fourth-and-goal from the 1. He pitched out to Alan Ameche, who had the option to pass the ball to tight end Jim Mutscheller. Instead, instinctive linebacker Cliff Livingston dragged Ameche down at the 5.

The Giants took possession and moved the ball to the 12 on runs by Gifford and Webster, setting the stage for the Giants' play of the day. Conerly faked a pitch to

Gifford and dropped back to pass under a heavy rush by Gino Marchetti. Conerly hit an open Kyle Rote crossing the 35. Rote broke a tackle by Carl Tasseff at the 48 and kept running until Andy Nelson grabbed him at the Colts' 40. With help from Ray Brown, Nelson wrestled Rote to the ground at the 35 as the ball came flying out.

While those three players scrambled to their feet, Alex Webster came rushing in from behind, scooped up the ball at the 25, and headed for the flag—but a hustling Tasseff knocked Alex out at the 1. On the next play after this 87-yard miracle, Mel Triplett dove in for the score, and the Giants were alive.

Baltimore could not move the ball, but Conerly was sharp on the Giants' next possession. Passes to Bob Schnelker moved the ball down the field, and a 15-yard strike to Gifford gave the Giants a 17–14 lead in the fourth period. The Colts missed another field goal, and the Giants had the ball with less than five minutes to play. They picked up one first down and were faced with a third-and-five from their 39 when they handed off to Gifford, who appeared to make the first down. However, Gino Marchetti's leg had been broken when teammate Big Daddy Lipscomb fell on the pile.

In the ensuing confusion of removing Marchetti on a stretcher, New York got a bad spot and faced fourth down. The players and offensive coach Vince Lombardi wanted to go for the first down, but Jim Lee Howell decided to punt. The rest is legend: a 62-yard drive in 1:53 for the tying field goal and a 13-play, 80-yard touchdown drive in overtime for the Colts victory.

The Colts were champions, and Johnny Unitas won a car as the game's MVP. Had Frank Gifford made that disputed first down, that car would have gone to Charley Conerly.

> It was the greatest game I've ever seen.
> —NFL COMMISSIONER BERT BELL

Frank Gifford (left), Mel Triplett (33), and Alex Webster (29) combined for an 87-yard pass play and subsequent touchdown run—unfortunately for the Giants, it wasn't enough to top the Colts.

September 20, 1964

Tittle Toppled

Steelers and Age Conquer Giants

From 1961 through 1963, the Giants lost one of the first two games of the season and recovered to win the East handily each year. So when New York dropped its 1964 opener to a blitzing Eagles team that sacked quarterback Y. A. Tittle five times—causing him to fumble three times and throw two interceptions—it was cause for concern but not panic. After all, Allie Sherman's teams had never lost two in a row. After the next game, though, against the Steelers, it was time to admit the obvious: the dynasty was crumbling.

All appeared well at the outset of this September day. Thirty-five-year-old Steelers quarterback Ed Brown got off to a slow start, throwing two interceptions in his first five passes. Erich Barnes returned one for a touchdown and a quick Giants lead. A 64-yard pass from 38-year-old Y. A. Tittle to 29-year-old Del Shofner led to a touchdown run by 33-year-old Alex Webster and a 14–0 first-period lead. However, the second quarter brought devastation.

As halftime approached, Tittle called an ill-fated screen pass from deep in his territory. While Tittle looked left for Joe Morrison, Steelers defensive end John Baker slipped by second-year tackle Lane Howell and came free.

Perhaps the most famous photograph in pro football history, the image of a bloody Tittle captures the rough, violent nature of the game. Ironically, the *Pittsburgh Post-Gazette* chose not to run the picture at the time because there was not enough action in it. It now hangs in the Pro Football Hall of Fame. (*Photo courtesy of AP Images*)

It looked like my head was hurting, but it was actually my rib cage. I pulled cartilage there. My head was bleeding because my helmet cut it when I hit the ground.

—Y. A. TITTLE, QUOTED IN *THE NEW YORK TIMES*

Baker crashed full-bore into Tittle's right side, with his forearm hitting Y. A. in the mouth and knocking off the quarterback's helmet. The force of the blow lifted Tittle off the ground as he floated a wounded-duck pass that defensive tackle Chuck Hinton gathered in at the 8-yard line and ran in for the score.

A dazed Tittle knelt in the end zone with a bloodied head and no helmet. This sad image was captured by local photographer Morris Berman, who won a National Headliner Award for the affecting shot. Tittle was unable to breathe and was helped to the locker room with bruised ribs.

The Steelers missed the extra point and kicked off to the Giants, who were now led by rookie scrambler Gary Wood. With a minute to go in the half, Wood was picked off by corner Brady Keys, which led to a second Pittsburgh score right before the intermission.

Both teams engineered long scoring drives in the third quarter to keep the game close. Pittsburgh's Brady Keys then set up the winning score in the final period with a

John Baker unloads a devastating hit on Y. A. Tittle, which caused Tittle to throw an interception on which Chuck Hinton scored. *(Photo courtesy of AP Images)*

Y. A. Tittle

Y. A. Tittle began his career in the All-America Football Conference with the original Baltimore Colts. He then spent a decade in San Francisco as part of the 49ers' "Million-Dollar Backfield" with Joe Perry, Hugh McElhenny, and John Henry Johnson. Tittle was a very precise passer with a sidearm throwing motion. In 1961, the 49ers shifted to the shotgun offense and felt they had no need for a 35-year-old quarterback, so they traded Tittle to New York for forgettable lineman Lou Cordileone.

Tittle came into a difficult situation in New York—supplanting respected veteran Charley Conerly—but ultimately his leadership brought the whole team together. Tittle led the aging Giants to three straight NFL Championship Games from 1961 to 1963; he won Player of the Year recognition each year. In those three years, Tittle threw for 86 touchdowns, including a record 33 in 1962 and a record 36 the following season. In the two latter seasons, he threw for more than 3,000 yards and ran the best passing offense in the NFL. The Giants lost all three title games, however, and then time ran out on Tittle and the team in 1964. Despite his brief time in blue, the Giants retired Tittle's No. 14 jersey because of his unequalled passing.

90-yard punt return. Keys was knocked out at the 1, but Ed Brown scored from there to put the Steelers up 27–21. Don Chandler added a 22-yard field goal, but he also missed one from the 37 to go with his two 42-yard misses from the first half.

New York was now 0–2 with an injured quarterback who suddenly looked old and feeble. Tittle would relieve Wood the following week against Washington and spark a victory, but he was injured again in the process. Although Tittle gamely would play in every game in 1964, the team finished the season 2–10–2. The championship run was over.

> **T**his is a moment I have dreaded. I don't want to come back and be a mediocre football player again. I was one last fall.
>
> —Y. A. TITTLE,
> FOUR MONTHS LATER AT HIS RETIREMENT

Game Details

New York Giants 24 • Pittsburgh Steelers 27

Giants	14	0	7	3	**24**
Steelers	0	13	7	7	**27**

Date: September 20, 1964

Team Records: Giants 0–1, Steelers 1–0

Scoring Plays:

NYG Barnes 26-yard interception return (Chandler PAT)

NYG Webster 2-yard run (Chandler PAT)

PIT Hinton 8-yard interception return (Clark kick failed)

PIT Johnson 2-yard pass from Brown (Clark PAT)

PIT Brown 2-yard run (Clark PAT)

NYG James 2-yard run (Chandler PAT)

PIT Brown 1-yard run (Clark PAT)

NYG Chandler 22-yard FG

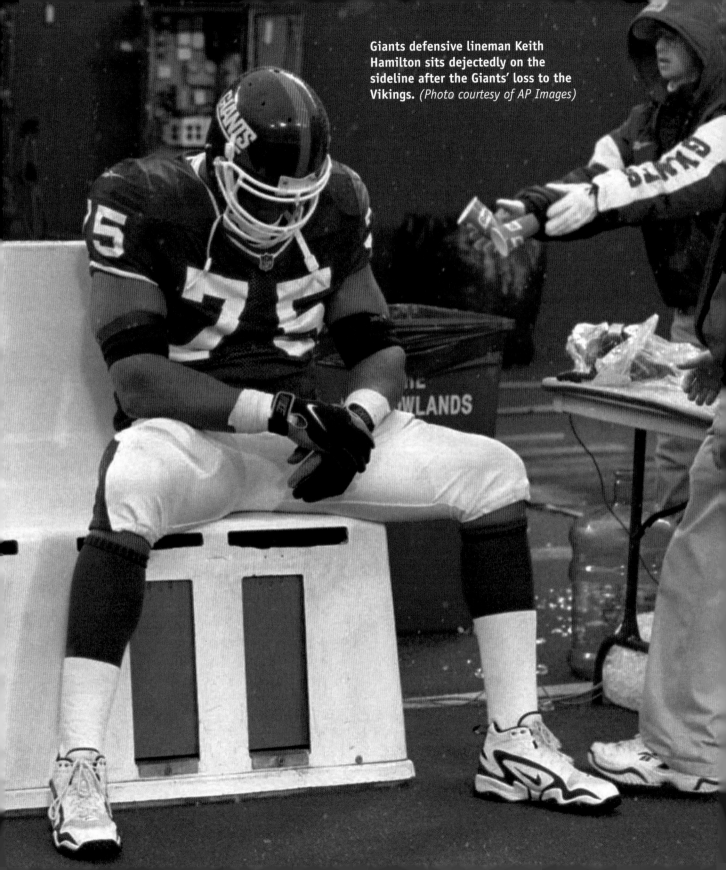

Giants defensive lineman Keith Hamilton sits dejectedly on the sideline after the Giants' loss to the Vikings. *(Photo courtesy of AP Images)*

Sure-Handed Calloway Lets Season Slip Through His Fingers

Vikings Oust Giants in Playoffs

In Jim Fassel's first year as coach, the Giants surprised everyone by rebounding from a 6–10 season to become 10–5–1 division champs in 1997. The team's success was built on a solid defense and a careful ball-control offense that relied on a committee of runners made up of Charles Way, Tiki Barber, and Tyrone Wheatley. In the playoffs, these overachievers were done in by mistakes and a loss of poise in a sloppy game in which the Vikings scored 10 points in the final 90 seconds.

At the outset, it was Minnesota making mistakes, but the Giants failed to fully capitalize. Two Randall Cunningham fumbles in the first quarter were recovered by the Giants and led to field goals. In the second quarter, a short punt by Minnesota gave New York good field position, and they drove 56 yards to score on a two-yard pass from Danny Kanell to tight end Aaron Pierce. Cunningham was then intercepted by Jason Sehorn, and that led to another field goal and a 16–0 lead with five minutes left in the first half. An Amani Toomer fumbled punt allowed Minnesota to get on the board with a field goal in the last two minutes. However, when Mitch Berger's kickoff went out of bounds, the Giants had great field position. Brad Daluiso then kicked a 51-yard field goal to end the half up 19–3.

Danny Kanell and the Quarterback Market

Jim Fassel said after the Minnesota game that Danny Kanell was his starter for the next season: "Danny managed the game well, and I expect him to take that to the next level." That was wishful thinking. One of the hidden reasons that the Giants lost to the Vikings was that they could not do any better than field goals, even with Minnesota's mistakes in the first half. On the first score, Kanell twice overthrew open receivers in the end zone before settling for the three-pointer. But how much could be expected of a fourth-round draft pick? The only reason that Kanell was the starter was that former first-round pick Dave Brown was a total flop.

The Giants have spent a No. 1 draft pick on a quarterback a total of five times. Philip Rivers was traded, but of the other four who stayed with the team, only Phil Simms was a success; Brown, Travis Tidwell, and Lee Grosscup were all busts. As a matter of fact, of the 10 other starting quarterbacks the Giants have drafted over the years, only third-rounders Jeff Hostetler and Don Heinrich have had any success. Kanell, Jesse Palmer, Randy Dean, Scott Brunner, Kent Graham, Bobby Clatterbuck, Jerry Golsteyn, and Gary Wood are all best forgotten.

The Giants have had much more luck in trading for quarterbacks. Since World War II, New York has obtained Frankie Filchock, Charley Conerly, Y. A. Tittle, Earl Morrall, Fran Tarkenton, and Eli Manning through trades. Of course, not all trades can be winners; other deals brought in lesser lights Norm Snead, Craig Morton, Jim Del Gaizo, George Shaw, Ralph Guglielmi, Milt Plum, Dick Shiner, and Randy Johnson.

The other avenue for quarterbacks—free agency—has also proven a mixed bag, bringing to New York Joe Pisarcik from the CFL, Kerry Collins and Tommy Maddox from the scrap heap, and Kurt Warner from a heroic recent past.

In the second half, the Giants began to implode. A Tiki Barber fumble on the New York 4-yard line led to a Vikings touchdown on the next play late in the third quarter, but the Giants still led by nine. A 14-yard Brad Maynard punt led to another Minnesota field goal at the start of the fourth quarter. Even more disturbing was an on-field argument between Giants defensive backs Phillippi Sparks and Conrad Hamilton in the midst of that drive that led to a physical confrontation between Sparks, Hamilton, and linebacker Jesse Armstead on the sideline. Meanwhile, defensive ends Michael Strahan and Keith Hamilton were going at it themselves, both on the field and off. New York still answered that field goal with the best drive of the day—13 plays covering 74 yards—and Daluiso nailed his fifth field goal to restore the nine-point lead, 22–13, with seven minutes left.

A few minutes later, a 26-yard punt by Brad Maynard gave Minnesota the ball on the New York 49. Two Cunningham passes—19 yards to Cris Carter and a 30-yard score to Jake Reed—pulled the Vikings within two. With the onside kick coming, the Giants put their best ball handlers on the field for what proved to be the most disappointing play of the game. Kicker Eddie Murray dribbled the ball to his left. New York's best and most sure-handed receiver, Chris Calloway, had the first shot at the ball 10 yards downfield, but shockingly, he let it bounce off his chest, and in the ensuing scramble the Vikings recovered it.

> It came up low. I knew the ground was wet, and it could skid and go fast. As I went down on it at the last minute, it kind of popped up. A football isn't like a baseball where you can scoop it up, but I should have had it, really.
>
> —CHRIS CALLOWAY

The Giants were reeling and continued to lose their composure, allowing Minnesota to drive down the field on seven plays, aided by an interference call on Sparks. Murray kicked the game-winning 24-yard field goal with 10 seconds remaining, and the Giants' season was over.

The internal squabbling would continue as a theme for the rest of Fassel's inconsistent seven-year tenure, although he would lead New York to one Super Bowl. Sadly, this spectacle was the last game for two Giants heroes. On the field, all-time leading rusher Rodney Hampton gained a paltry 18 yards in his final appearance; watching from a booth above was the man responsible for the turnaround of the Giants franchise over the last two decades, retiring general manager George Young.

Game Details

New York Giants 22 • Minnesota Vikings 23

Vikings	0	3	7	13	**23**
Giants	6	13	0	3	**22**

Date: December 27, 1997

Team Records: Giants 10–5–1, Vikings 9–7

Scoring Plays:

NYG Daluiso 43-yard FG

NYG Daluiso 22-yard FG

NYG Pierce 2-yard pass from Kanell (Daluiso PAT)

NYG Daluiso 41-yard FG

MIN Murray 26-yard FG

NYG Daluiso 51-yard FG

MIN Hoard 4-yard run (Murray PAT)

MIN Murray 26-yard FG

NYG Daluiso 22-yard FG

MIN Reed 30-yard pass from Cunningham (Murray PAT)

MIN Murray 24-yard FG

Vikings kicker Eddie Murray celebrates his game-winning field goal as Giants defensive back Percy Ellsworth walks dejectedly off the field. Ellsworth was one of two New York players who failed to recover Murray's onside kick a few moments earlier. *(Photo courtesy of AP Images)*

The Hit Heard 'Round the World

Gifford and Giants Fall to Eagles

Having won three of four Eastern Conference titles, the Giants looked well-positioned to make another run in Week 8 of the 1960 season. The 6–1 Eagles were in town for a first-place showdown with the 5–1–1 Giants, and New York got off to a good start with a 10–0 halftime lead on a Joe Morrison touchdown run and a Pat Summerall field goal. At the half, the Giants had 12 first downs versus four for the Eagles, and Philadelphia quarterback Norm Van Brocklin was under constant pressure from the Giants defense, which held him to just one completion in six attempts.

To stabilize the Eagles' front line, veteran linebacker Chuck Bednarik replaced rookie center Bill Lapham for the second half, telling Giants linebacker Sam Huff that the "men were taking over now." This would be the first of several games in which Bednarik would play both ways during the Eagles' stretch drive. The bolstered Eagles offense evened up the game on a 35-yard touchdown pass to Tommy McDonald in the third quarter and a Bobby Walston field goal in the fourth quarter.

With the score tied at 10–10, the Giants got the ball back behind quarterback George Shaw, who was subbing for an injured Charley Conerly. Facing a third-and-inches at their 38-yard line, Shaw handed off to fullback Mel Triplett, but the exchange was shaky and when Triplett was hit by Bednarik at the line of scrimmage, the ball popped up in the air. Safety Jimmy Carr snatched it and raced untouched into the end zone for a 17–10 Eagles lead with 2:33 to play.

With the situation now desperate, Shaw hit Gifford for a 33-yard gain to midfield. Shaw overthrew Gifford on his next pass and then sent Bob Schnelker deep on second down. Schnelker was open and Shaw was on target, but the normally reliable receiver let the ball fall right through his hands.

Next came the play of the day. Needing a first down on third-and-10, Shaw went back to the team's leader, Gifford, and hit him near the right hash mark at the Eagles' 35. With two Eagles converging from the front and Bednarik circling from behind, Gifford attempted to cut back behind Bednarik.

In perhaps the most famous tackle in NFL history, Bednarik hit Gifford hard and high, knocking him backward off his feet so that his head bounced off the frozen field, rendering Gifford unconscious. In the process, Gifford fumbled and Chuck Weber of Philadelphia recovered the ball. When

Eagles linebacker Chuck Bednarik knocks Frank Gifford unconscious in one of the most famous and brutal plays in football history.

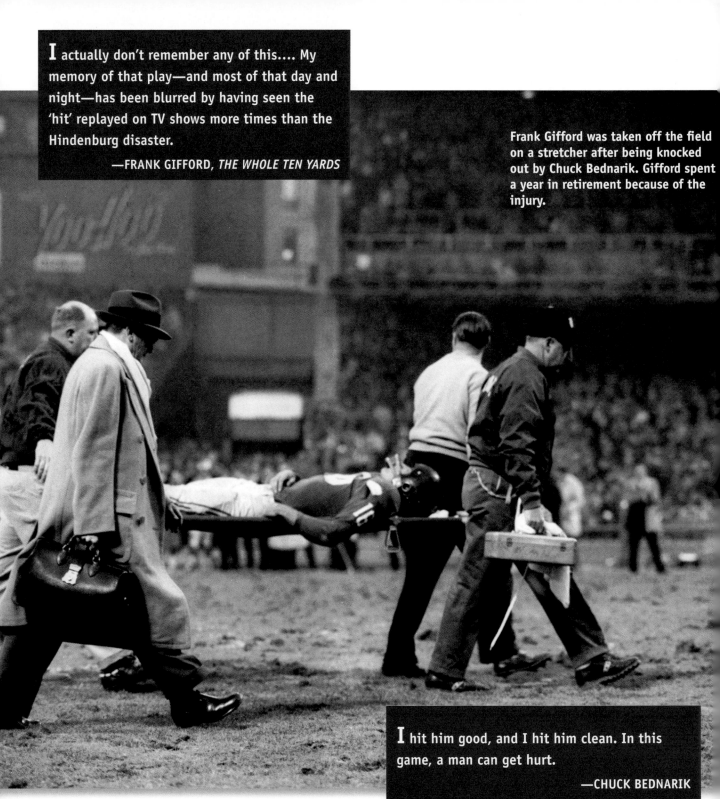

I actually don't remember any of this.... My memory of that play—and most of that day and night—has been blurred by having seen the 'hit' replayed on TV shows more times than the Hindenburg disaster.

—FRANK GIFFORD, *THE WHOLE TEN YARDS*

Frank Gifford was taken off the field on a stretcher after being knocked out by Chuck Bednarik. Gifford spent a year in retirement because of the injury.

I hit him good, and I hit him clean. In this game, a man can get hurt.

—CHUCK BEDNARIK

Frank Gifford

Chuck Bednarik knocked Frank Gifford clear into another season with his concussion-inducing smackdown. The 30-year-old Gifford went into retirement in 1961, but he missed the action and was eager to return in 1962, when he replaced his old teammate Kyle Rote as the Giants' dependable flanker for three more years.

Handsome and stylish, Gifford was an early pop-culture icon who moved easily in the bright lights on and off the field. He inspired hero worship from many fans—most notably troubled writer Frederick Exley, whose novel *A Fan's Notes* used Gifford and the Giants as a prism through which he viewed his own life.

Gifford was a Southern California native who starred as an All-American tailback at USC, and he also did some acting. He was the top pick of New York in 1952, but Giants coach Steve Owen was suspicious of Gifford and primarily used him on defense. Under new offensive coach Vince Lombardi, though, Gifford's career changed course in his third year. Lombardi valued Gifford's "versatility and alertness" and used his running, receiving, and passing abilities as the centerpiece of New York's offense. In 1956, the Giants won the title and Gifford won the league MVP award.

When he retired for good in 1964, Gifford was first in team history in points, touchdowns, and receiving yards and second in receptions and rushing yards.

Gifford was elected to the Hall of Fame in 1977 and had his number retired by the Giants in 2000. In a high-profile second career, he spent more than 30 years as a broadcaster, most notably on *Monday Night Football* with Howard Cosell and Don Meredith.

Bednarik saw that, he leaped in the air to celebrate winning the game, but all the Giants and their fans saw was a cocky brute taunting their fallen star. The Giants' 5'5" team doctor screamed expletives at Bednarik, and quarterback Conerly called him a "cheap-shot artist," but the hit was clean and brutal.

In a bit of quirky scheduling, the teams met again the following week in Philadelphia. Once again, the Giants got off to a lead—17–0 in the first quarter this time—but could not hold it. The Eagles were in the midst of a magical season in which six of their 10 victories would be comeback wins. The Giants, by contrast, were headed to a 6–4–2 third-place finish and were starting to look old. A new coach, quarterback, and wide receiver would turn the club around in 1961, but Frank Gifford would retire and spend that season as a team scout while he began his broadcasting career.

Game Details

New York Giants 10 • Philadelphia Eagles 17

Eagles	0	0	7	10	**17**
Giants	7	3	0	0	**10**

Date: November 20, 1960

Team Records: Giants 5–1–1, Eagles 6–1

Scoring Plays:

NYG Morrison 1-yard run (Summerall PAT)

NYG Summerall 26-yard FG

PHL McDonald 35-yard pass from Van Brocklin (Walston PAT)

PHL Walston 12-yard FG

PHL Carr 38-yard fumble recovery (Walston PAT)

January 5, 2003

Season Ends in a Snap

Giants Lose to 49ers on a Botched Field-Goal Attempt

On a sunny afternoon of big plays, big leads, big comebacks, and bigger mental and physical lapses from both sides of the field, this NFC Wild-Card Game came down to the simplest of plays with six seconds remaining: a medium-length field goal. Unfortunately, the Giants botched it for the second time in three minutes. However, as several players noted after the game, it never should have gotten to that point.

The 49ers struck first in this wild contest, with a 76-yard touchdown pass to Terrell Owens on their first play, five minutes into the first quarter. The Giants answered with a 12-yard touchdown pass to Amani Toomer, one of three scores Toomer would grab during the afternoon. Quarterback Kerry Collins hit Jeremy Shockey for a two-yard score just three minutes later, but the 49ers responded with a Kevan Barlow touchdown run to tie the score at 14–14.

The Giants took control of the game before halftime with two more Collins-to-Toomer touchdowns, of eight and 24 yards, in the last three minutes of the half; they went to the locker room with a 28–14 lead. New York continued its dominance in the third quarter with a Tiki Barber touchdown run and a Matt Bryant 21-yard field goal to stretch the lead to 38–14 with less than 20 minutes to play.

Down 24 points, the 49ers went to a no-huddle offense that put additional pressure on the tiring Giants defensive line, which was unable to substitute players because of the faster pace. With two minutes left in the quarter, Jeff Garcia hit Owens for a 24-yard touchdown, and followed that with a two-point conversion on which Garcia scrambled to buy time for Owens to get open. Still leading 38–22, New York's offense went three-and-out, and the Giants were forced to punt from their own 12-yard line. Matt Allen delivered a lame 30-yard punt that Vinny Sutherland of the 49ers caught at the New York 42, as Dhani Jones plowed into him on a boneheaded play for which the Giants were penalized 15 yards.

Starting at the New York 27, San Francisco scored quickly on a 14-yard scramble on the first play of the fourth quarter. Another scramble on the two-point conversion allowed Garcia to find Owens again to make the score 38–30 with just under 15 minutes to play. Once again, the Giants offense was forced to punt after just three unsuccessful plays, and the 49ers drove down the field and

A botched snap and a pass interference call that never came left Rich Seubert (69) and the Giants dazed and confused in a wild 39–38 playoff loss to the 49ers in 2003. *(Photo courtesy of AP Images)*

Quarterback Kerry Collins stares in disbelief after the Giants fell to the 49ers 39–38. *(Photo courtesy of AP Images)*

kicked a field goal halfway through the quarter to make the score 38–33.

Finally, the Giants offense woke up and marched from their 36 to the 49ers' 24. On fourth-and-one, coach Jim Fassel elected to go for the easy 42-yard field goal that would restore their eight-point lead with 3:06 to go. In an ominous bit of foreshadowing, newly signed veteran long-snapper Trey Junkin fired a bad snap that holder Matt Allen was barely able to get down, and a confused Matt Bryant missed the kick to the left. From their 32, the 49ers moved down the field again on the legs and arm of Jeff Garcia, who hit Tai Streets for a 13-yard touchdown to take a 39–38 lead with 1:05 to play. Will Allen intercepted the two-point conversion intended again for Terrell

Game Details

New York Giants 38 • San Francisco 49ers 39

Giants	7	21	10	0	**38**
49ers	7	7	8	17	**39**

Date: January 5, 2003

Team Records: Giants 10–6, 49ers 10–6

Scoring Plays:

SF	Owens 76-yard pass from Garcia (Chandler PAT)
NYG	Toomer 12-yard pass from Collins (Bryant PAT)
NYG	Shockey 2-yard pass from Collins (Bryant PAT)
SF	Barlow 1-yard run (Chandler PAT)
NYG	Toomer 8-yard pass from Collins (Bryant PAT)
NYG	Toomer 24-yard pass from Collins (Bryant PAT)
NYG	Barber 6-yard run (Bryant PAT)
NYG	Bryant 21-yard FG
SF	Owens 26-yard pass from Garcia (Owens pass from Garcia)
SF	Garcia 14-yard run (Owens pass from Garcia)
SF	Chandler 25-yard FG
SF	Streets 13-yard pass from Garcia (pass failed)

Owens, and Owens flung Allen out of bounds, drawing a flag for unnecessary roughness. However, Giants safety Shaun Williams retaliated against Owens and drew his own offsetting penalty, so the Giants would get no advantage on the ensuing kickoff.

Despite this mental error, the Giants got a big return from Delvin Joyce and started at their own 48 with one minute left. Kerry Collins went to work and hit Ron Dixon twice before missing Toomer. With six seconds left, Collins hit Toomer on a five-yard out at the 23 to set up the potential 41-yard winning field goal.

The field-goal unit came onto the field. Allen told Bryant to trust him and expect the ball to be down despite the bad snap of three minutes before. Allen then told Junkin, the snapper, "You've been in this league for 19 years; you've got to come through for us." Once the team was set, Allen called for the ball, and Junkin squirted the ball low and so far to the right that Allen grabbed it, rose up, and yelled "Fire" to his teammates to signal a broken play.

Allen rolled out with 49ers in pursuit as guard Rich Seubert, an eligible receiver on this play, went out for a pass. Allen unloaded the ball in the direction of Seubert, who was open at the 2-yard line, but Chidi Okeafor of the 49ers tackled Seubert as penalty flags flew and the pass fell incomplete. To the amazement of everyone, the Giants were called for having an ineligible receiver downfield because guard Tam Hopkins was also inexplicably at the goal line, but interference was not called on Okeafor so there were no offsetting penalties, and the game was over.

Two months earlier in Arizona, Junkin had been interviewed for a piece in *Sports Illustrated* in which he described the anonymous nature of his long, strange career: "Ideally, my name should never come up. If it does, I've made a mistake," he said. Unfortunately, Junkin did just that on the immense stage of the NFL playoffs.

One day later, the NFL admitted its officiating error and said that interference should have been called and that the offsetting penalties should have resulted in a rekick for New York.

TIKI'S take

Going into this playoff matchup, we had won seven of our last nine games. Jim Fassel had taken over the play calling from Sean Payton, and our offense was explosive in that stretch, averaging 26 points per game. That's how this game went for the first 42 minutes; we were up 38–14 with just three minutes to go in the third quarter when the 49ers started making plays of their own. You're really only as good as your weakest link, and our weakest link that year was our kicking game. We did a lot of great things, but when the 49ers needed stops, they got them; when we needed stops, we didn't. This loss hurt a lot because we knew we should have won. The next week, San Francisco lost to Tampa Bay, and the Bucs went on to win it all. At least my brother Ronde got his Super Bowl ring.

It just got away from us; it was tragic. In the end, what got us was what I worried about from the start of the season: snap, hold, kick.

—JIM FASSEL

December 17, 1933

Sleight of Hand, Misdirection, and Who's Got the Ball?

Giants Come Up One Trick Short Against the Bears

The very first NFL Championship Game in 1933 has seldom been equaled in the ensuing seasons of title games and Super Bowls. The game featured six lead changes, and all five touchdowns were set up or scored on passing plays, highly unusual for this ground-oriented era. During the season, New York scored the most points and the Bears gained the most yards in the league, and both won their conference crown by at least three games. They were the two best teams in the NFL by far, and they proved it on this cold, misty day in Wrigley Field.

Early on, the Giants set the quirky tempo for this game with the trickiest play of the day. They lined up with only an end to the left of center Mel Hein. Before the ball was snapped, that end dropped back into the backfield as a wingback, while the wingback on the right side shifted up to the line. According to the rules of the time, Hein was now an eligible receiver. Hein hiked the ball to

Harry Newman, who slid the ball right back to the center. Pretending to have the ball, Newman dropped back to pass and the Bears defense followed. When George Musso tackled Newman, he bellowed, "Where the hell's the ball?" Meanwhile, Hein hid the ball under his shirt and started slowly downfield, but he quickly got impatient and began running. Bears safety Keith Molesworth saw through the trick and brought Hein down after a gain of several yards.

That drive led to no points, though. Instead, the Bears got on the board first after a Bronko Nagurski interception in the first quarter led to a Jack Manders field goal. The Bears then got a second field goal after another drive in the second quarter. The Giants finally answered with a drive of their own that ended with a 29-yard touchdown pass from Newman to Red Badgro for the first lead change of the day. Manders missed a short field-goal try just before halftime, and the Giants went to the locker room leading 7–6.

Manders kicked his third field goal in the third period to take the lead back, but Newman's passes to Dale Burnett, Kink Richards, and Max Krause brought New York to the

Chicago 1-yard line. Krause punched it in from there to put the Giants in the lead again 14–9.

On their next possession, the Bears used a trick play of their own. George Corbett faked a punt and instead threw a pass to quarterback Carl Brumbaugh; the play traveled 67 yards to the Giants' 8. From there, Nagurski threw a jump pass to Bill Karr for the touchdown and a 16–14 lead at the end of three quarters.

The Giants continued passing and got to the Bears' 8, where a broken play produced another touchdown and lead change. Ken Strong took a handoff from Newman and tried to head around the left end. Seeing nothing but Bears defenders, Strong improvised and tossed the ball back to a surprised Newman. As the Bears charged for Newman, Strong drifted into the end zone, where the retreating Newman spotted him and hit him for a touchdown in an unplanned flea flicker.

No amount of offensive trickery could push the Giants past Bill Hewitt (lateraling) and the Bears in the 1933 NFL Championship Game.

The idea was to just walk down the field. I took four to five steps, and I got excited and took off running. I made it about 30 yards.
—MEL HEIN, IN *THE NFL'S TOP 40* BY SHELBY STROTHER

Mel Hein's hidden-ball trick momentarily fooled the Chicago Bears during the first NFL Championship Game.

Harry Newman

The hidden-ball play the Giants ran in this first NFL Championship Game originated, oddly enough, with the nieces of tailback Harry Newman. He was watching them play a touch football game in which they had the quarterback hand the ball back to the center, and that got Harry thinking. He discussed it with coach Steve Owen, and they sprung the trick play on the Bears.

Harry grew up in Detroit and attended Benny Friedman's summer camp, where Friedman taught him how to pass and recommended him to his alma mater, the University of Michigan. The Giants signed the 5'8" passer upon his graduation in 1933.

As a rookie, Newman led the league in passing yards, with 973, and in touchdowns, with 11—as well as in attempts, completions, and yards. He also finished sixth in the NFL in rushing. In the championship game, he threw for 201 yards, an astonishing total for the time. The rookie sensation fell victim to a sophomore slump, though, falling to just one touchdown pass and averaging just four yards per completion in 1934. His second season ended early when his back was injured by the crush of the Bears' pass rush during a regular-season game. Ed Danowski took over as tailback, led the Giants to the title, and then kept the starting job the following season.

Trailing in the closing minutes of the game, Chicago got the ball in great field position after a poor punt by Strong. After a couple of runs, Nagurski tried another jump pass and completed it to Bill Hewitt, who then lateraled the ball to a trailing Bill Karr at the 19. Karr went in for the winning score. The strange thing was that the lowly Philadelphia Eagles had utilized the very same hook-and-lateral play for a touchdown against the Giants just one week before. New York should have been prepared for it.

The Giants still had time left for two plays, and they tried two more tricks. On the first, they lined up as they had for Hein's earlier hidden-ball play. However, this time Newman took the snap and pitched out to Dale Burnett. As the Bears pursued Burnett, Hein sped downfield as a wide-open receiver, but Burnett was quickly swarmed over and his weak pass was batted down. On the final play, New York tried their own hook-and-lateral play, but the Bears' Red Grange wrapped up receiver Red Badgro so that he was unable to lateral the ball to the trailing Burnett. The game was over; the Bears were champions, but the Giants could hold their heads high and plan for a better outcome next year.

Game Details

New York Giants 21 • Chicago Bears 23

Giants	0	7	7	7	**21**
Bears	3	3	10	7	**23**

Date: December 17, 1933

Team Records: Giants 11–3, Bears 10–2–1

Scoring Plays:

CHI Manders 16-yard FG

CHI Manders 40-yard FG

NYG Badgro 29-yard pass from Newman (Strong PAT)

CHI Manders 28-yard FG

NYG Krause 1-yard run (Strong PAT)

CHI Karr 8-yard pass from Nagurski (Manders PAT)

NYG Strong 8-yard pass from Newman (Strong PAT)

CHI Karr 19-yard lateral from Hewitt after 14-yard pass from Nagurski (Brumbaugh PAT)

December 30, 2001

Lambuth Special Stopped Short of the Playoffs

Time Runs Out for Giants Against Eagles

A spectacular play the Giants hadn't practiced since training camp nearly kept their expiring postseason hopes alive on the final play of a hard-fought battle with division rival Philadelphia—but it fell a few yards short of the mark. After 2000's surprising Super Bowl appearance, the play called "86 Lambuth Special" served as a fitting metaphor for the Giants' disappointing, oh-so-close 2001 season, in which they missed the playoffs by losing three games in the last minutes by a total of just five points to the Eagles and the Rams.

Going into this 15th game of the year, 7–7 New York trailed the 9–5 Eagles by two games, but a victory in Philadelphia would keep the Giants' postseason hopes alive. October's 10–9 loss to the Eagles at the Meadowlands had broken the Giants' nine-game winning streak over Philadelphia; it was the first time Jim Fassel had lost to the Eagles or to their coach, Andy Reid.

With control of the division on the line the night before New Year's Eve, tempers were short and players from the opposing teams got into a scuffle during warm-ups, 45 minutes before the game even started. The Eagles opened the game with a 72-yard drive that culminated in a five-yard touchdown pass from Donovan McNabb to Chad Lewis. The remainder of the first half was a hard-hitting defensive contest, in which Michael Strahan continued his mastery over Eagles tackle Jon Runyan by constantly harrassing McNabb. Strahan had 3.5 sacks in the first half and had many big plays throughout the game.

The Giants evened the score at the outset of the second half with a flea flicker in which Tiki Barber took a handoff from Kerry Collins and tossed the ball back to the quarterback, who then hit Amani Toomer for a 60-yard touchdown. Later in the quarter, a 30-yard Ron Dayne run led to a 25-yard

Tiki Barber's lateral to Ron Dixon on the 86 Lambuth Special wasn't enough to save the Giants against the Eagles in the 2001 regular-season finale.

TIKI'S take

In 2000, we made it to the Super Bowl but were shut down by Ray Lewis and the Baltimore Ravens. The 2001 season, though, was one of great disappointment and near misses. We came into this game against the 9–5 Eagles with a 7–7 record, but having lost to both Philadelphia and St. Louis by a single point. The Eagles scored the last 10 points to pull ahead by three with just seven seconds to play, and with one last chance to save our season Coach Fassel called for the Lambuth Special from our own 20-yard line. The play was supposed to first go to Ike Hilliard who would then lateral to me, and then I would make a second pitch to speedy Ron Dixon running in the opposite direction of all the Eagles defenders. When Kerry Collins couldn't get the ball to Hilliard, though, he came directly to me. I couldn't locate Dixon, so I tossed the ball where I thought he would be. Despite the confusion, Ron grabbed the ball and took off. No one touched him for 60 yards until he ran out of room at the Eagles' 6-yard line as time expired. Falling just short, the play was a microcosm of our whole frustrating season.

field goal, giving the Giants a 10–7 lead going into the exciting fourth quarter.

The Eagles took the lead back in the first minute of the final quarter on a 57-yard bomb from McNabb to speedster James Thrash. The Giants answered with a field goal to draw within a point; they then drove 81 yards and scored on a 16-yard run by Dayne. New York went for two, and Tiki Barber's successful two-point conversion gave the Giants a 21–14 lead with 2:43 to play.

McNabb responded by driving the Eagles 67 yards in six plays, including a 32-yard reception by Thrash, with Lewis again catching the scoring pass with 1:49 remaining. Philadelphia used all their timeouts and forced a three-and-out from the Giants. Starting at their 29-yard line with 58 seconds left, the Eagles marched 54 yards in seven plays to the Giants' 17, where David Akers kicked a 35-yard field goal to take the lead with seven seconds

Game Details

New York Giants 21 • Philadelphia Eagles 24

Giants	0	0	10	11	**21**
Eagles	7	0	0	17	**24**

Date: December 30, 2001

Team Records: Giants 7–7, Eagles 9–5

Scoring Plays:

PHL Lewis 5-yard pass from McNabb (Akers PAT)

NYG Toomer 60-yard pass from Collins (Andersen PAT)

NYG Andersen 25-yard FG

PHL Thrash 57-yard pass from McNabb (Akers PAT)

NYG Andersen 32-yard FG

NYG Dayne 16-yard run (Barber run)

PHL Lewis 7-yard pass from McNabb (Akers PAT)

PHL Akers 35-yard FG

Jesse Armstead

Jesse Armstead manfully and correctly stated after the game, "I had no idea where [Dixon] was because I was still so pissed off. If something happened, if he scored a touchdown, great. But I was still so mad at how we came up short, I didn't really care. If I had an extra leg, I'd be kicking myself."

Armstead was so mad because not only had the Giants given up 17 fourth-quarter points, but 10 of them came in the last 1:49. The defense let the game slip away.

Armstead was a playmaker known for his intelligence, speed, and ball-hawking instincts during his nine years as a Giant.

This loss to the Eagles, though, would be Armstead's next-to-last game in blue. The aging veteran who correctly diagnosed the defense's weakness left for Washington as a free agent. After two years, Armstead re-signed with New York and immediately retired, a Giant forever.

Linebacker Jesse Armstead was a team leader and one of coach Jim Fassel's favorite players during his years with the Giants.

to play. The key plays on the drive were a 25-yard strike to Thrash and a clock-stopping five-yard delay-of-game penalty against Michael Strahan for not letting Donovan McNabb get up after Strahan tackled him just one play before the field goal.

Down 24–21 with seven seconds left, it appeared the Giants had no hope after the touchback on the ensuing kickoff gave them the ball at their own 20. Fassel ordered the 86 Lambuth Special, named after the small Tennessee school that speedster Ron Dixon had attended. The Lambuth Special is nothing more than a variation on the old hook-and-lateral play that has been around since the dawn of pro football. Kerry Collins took the snap and threw a seven-yard pass to Tiki Barber on the left. As Barber and his blockers headed right, Ron Dixon crossed behind Barber from the right and took a lateral at the 40, headed in the opposite direction from the Eagles' pursuit.

With all the Eagles defenders out of position, Dixon took off down the sideline with the end zone in his sights. As Dixon got closer to the sideline, he slowed down a bit, looking for a cutback lane, and was caught at the 6-yard line by the only Eagles player with a shot at him, safety Damon Moore. As Dixon was knocked out of bounds, the Giants looked up at the clock to see the sad sight of 0:00. The game—and the season—were over. General manager Ernie Accorsi summed it up by saying, "For what it meant and how we lost it, it was heartbreaking."

That's the most horrifying ending to a ball game I've ever seen.

—JOHN McVAY

After a botched exchange between Giants quarterback Joe Pisarcik and Larry Csonka, Eagles cornerback Herman Edwards pounces on the ill-timed fumble and returns it for the game-winning touchdown on November 19, 1978. *(Photo courtesy of AP Images)*

Coach's Blunder, Quarterback's Bobble

Giants Fumble Away Season to Eagles

In Philadelphia, the play is still called the "Miracle of the Meadowlands" more than 30 years later, but in New York it will forever be "the Fumble." In 1978, neither the Giants nor the Eagles had been in a playoff game for at least 15 years. In fact, the Giants' record from 1964 through 1977 was 68–124–4, while the Eagles achieved a nearly identical mark of 68–122–6. In 1978, New York and Philadelphia were stumbling around on the outskirts of playoff contention and came into this Week 12 game with 5–6 and 6–5 records, respectively. It came as a surprise that this clumsily played game would be a turning point for each ill-managed franchise.

New York got off to an early lead as bargain-basement quarterback "Parkway Joe" Pisarcik led the Giants on a nine-play, 72-yard drive, capped by a touchdown pass to Bobby Hammond halfway through the first quarter. Less than two minutes later, Brad Van Pelt intercepted a Ron Jaworski pass, and Pisarcik cashed in on a 30-yard strike to Johnny Perkins for a 14–0 lead.

The Eagles got back into the game with 1:26 left in the half when Wilbert Montgomery ran for an eight-yard touchdown. A bad snap on the extra point proved costly to Philadelphia; their kicker Nick Mike-Mayer was injured trying to throw a pass on the botched play. The Giants then moved into scoring position quickly, but Pisarcik was picked off in the end zone at the end of the first half.

Joe Danelo extended the Giants' lead to 17–6 in the third quarter, but the Eagles closed the gap with less than four minutes remaining in the lackluster game when Mike Hogan bulled in from the 1-yard line. The touchdown came after the Birds had driven 91 yards in 13 plays, aided

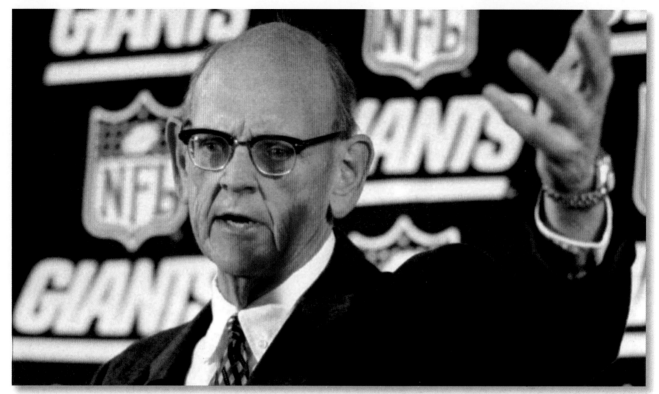

George Young ran the Giants' football operations from 1979 through 1998. *(Photo courtesy of AP Images)*

by three Giants penalties. Punter Mike Michel missed the extra point, and Philadelphia trailed 17–12.

Giants running back Doug Kotar fumbled the ball away at his 33 with 3:22 to play, but two minutes later cornerback Odis McKinney intercepted a Jaworski pass at the New York 10, seemingly preserving a victory that would leave both teams with 6–6 records. The Giants called three running plays and used up the Eagles' timeouts. With 31 seconds left in the game, New York faced a third-and-two at their own 28. All they had to do was snap the ball and have Pisarcik take a knee and the clock would run out.

None of the Giants' offensive players could believe that offensive coordinator Bob Gibson sent in a play that called for a handoff to fullback Larry Csonka, and several of them vociferously protested against it in the huddle. Pisarcik chose to follow orders, though. He took the handoff gripping the back end of the ball, and turned to the right before swinging all the way around to find Csonka, who was headed to Joe's left. The aborted handoff bounced off

Game Details

New York Giants 17 • Philadelphia Eagles 19

Eagles	0	6	0	13	**19**
Giants	14	0	3	0	**17**

Date: November 19, 1978

Team Records: Giants 5–6, Eagles 6–5

Scoring Plays:

NYG Hammond 19-yard pass from Pisarcik (Danelo PAT)

NYG Perkins 30-yard pass from Pisarcik (Danelo PAT)

PHL Montgomery 8-yard run (Mike-Mayer kick failed)

NYG Danelo 37-yard FG

PHL Hogan 1-yard run (Michel kick failed)

PHL Edwards 26-yard fumble recovery (Michel PAT)

George Young

Two years after Peter Finch won an Oscar for his role in the film *Network*, Giants fans empathized with his crazed character's catchphrase, "I'm mad as hell and I'm not going to take it anymore!" The day after "the Fumble," offensive coach Bob Gibson was fired. Two weeks later, 100 fans burned their tickets and mailed the ashes to owner Wellington Mara. The week after that, some fans rented a plane to fly a banner that read "15 Years of Lousy Football—We've Had Enough" over the stadium during the last home game of 1978.

The deleterious effect of this happening to one of the league's flagship franchises was not lost on NFL commissioner Pete Rozelle, who worked diligently behind the scenes to get Wellington Mara and his nephew Tim to put aside their feud and agree on a new general manager to restore the New York Giants to prominence. Finally, on Valentine's Day 1979, the Giants hired George Young to run their football operation.

Young had begun as a successful high school coach in Baltimore; he caught the eye of Don Shula, who hired him to work in scouting. Over the years, Young worked his way up in first the Colts and then the Dolphins organizations, mentored by Shula. The Dolphins' personnel director was ideally suited not only to rebuild the New York franchise through astute drafts and coaching hires, but also to serve as a resilient buffer between the two incompatible Maras. Young hired disciplinarian Ray Perkins as coach, and New York made the playoffs three years later. When Perkins decided to leave to replace the legendary Bear Bryant at his Alabama alma mater, Young replaced him with defensive coach Bill Parcells, and Parcells would complete the restoration by leading the Giants to two Super Bowl wins in eight seasons.

When Young decided to step down in 1998, he left a legacy of accomplishment, organization, honor, dignity, and integrity. He also left an in-house successor in Ernie Accorsi, who carried on in the Young style and maintained the overall success of the franchise.

Csonka's hip as he plowed into the line. Pisarcik dove for the bouncing ball, and Csonka turned around too late: Eagles cornerback Herman Edwards pushed through a weak block by Kotar and scooped up the ball as it bounced right into his hands. Edwards carried the ball triumphantly in his left hand as he sprinted the 26 yards to the end zone with tight end Gary Shirk in fruitless pursuit. Edwards's monster spike signaled an impossible Giants loss and the low point for the franchise.

New York would lose three of their last four games to finish 6–10, while the Eagles would split their last four and improbably make the playoffs. The victory validated coach Dick Vermeil's turnaround of the franchise and enabled them to make the postseason, but it also contained a poison pill in the loss of their kicker. Vermeil tried to make it work by using his punter to place-kick, but Michel missed an extra point and two chip-shot field goals in a one-point playoff loss to Atlanta.

New York had at last bottomed out, and a new general manager in 1979 would begin restoring the team's greatness.

> **I** don't know where that play came from.
>
> —LARRY CSONKA

Acknowledgments

I would like to thank a number of individuals who helped me with this book. First, thanks to Tiki Barber for generously contributing his foreword and sharing his memories and insights. Marcia Schiff and Matthew Lutts at AP Images and Christiana Newton and Tamyka Muse at Getty Images provided able assistance in researching photographs for the book. Mary Anne Nesbit at Rutgers University has always been helpful in borrowing obscure materials from other libraries. John Gibson, also at Rutgers, has helped me unfailingly with technology questions for many years now. A couple of Giants fans, Alan Ludwig and Dr. Ken Leistner, offered advice during the project. Finally, all the pros at Triumph Books made writing this book a delightful experience.